Table of Contents

D1404021

A Note About This Book

For most students, learning information in APUSH once during the course of the year is simply not enough considering the vast amount covered on the test. A good review is essential, which is why many teachers spend at least a few weeks before the test going back over as much as possible. A review book is also advisable for most to help them retool before the exam. However, I discovered very few of my students actually purchased a review book. Of the various free resources online, .pdf summaries or "most important info" examples, I found them all lacking and incomplete. Thus, the origins of this book.

This review is a concise, practical guide to U.S. History. One of the chief complaints I've heard about most commercial review books is that they're too long and that it's almost like reading the textbook over again. Much time has been spent considering what to include and what not to in this review guide. It is broken up essentially into two main parts: 1) a chronological history of the United States from the colonial era to the present and 2) a thematic/categorical section including excerpts from the chronological section synthesized into groups such as Women's history, Native American history, etc. as well as sections on political parties, amendments, Supreme Ct. decisions, and more. In addition, there are writing tips and a couple of sample essays included.

The book follows generally how I teach the class. I like to have fun in discussing history; I'd hate for students to think U.S. history is boring. Therefore you'll find the occasional comments in parentheses including using my favorite phrase, "scandalous," simply reflecting that what might sometimes seem boring on the page, was in fact exciting, interesting, and controversial.

Author Thanks

Thanks to Bill Shelton for giving me a great start to APUSH. Thanks to my wife and son putting up with all the time it took to complete this. And thanks to my many students over the years who have made this book worthwhile and made me want to remain an APUSH teacher. APUSH now, APUSH tomorrow, APUSH forever!

Cover Image: Washington Crossing the Delaware by Emanuel Gottlieb Leutze (1851)

APUSH Exam Info

The APUSH exam is made up of two parts: a 55-minute multiple-choice section and a 130-minute free-response section for a total test time of 3 hours and 5 minutes. The free-response section contains three parts (A,B,C) and begins with a mandatory 15-minute reading period. Students are usually recommended to spend most of the 15 minutes analyzing the documents and planning their answer to the document-based essay question (DBQ) in Part A. The rest of the 115 minutes is free for you to use as needed to complete the three essays. You must answer the DBQ in part A and it is usually recommended to spend about 45 minutes on this portion. Then you must select 1 (of 2) essay prompt from section B and 1 (of 2) essay prompt from section C. Essay topics may range from the early exploration and colonial era to the present, however, none of the prompts should deal exclusively with the period since 1980.

Both the multiple-choice and the free-response sections cover the period from the first European explorations of the Americas to the present, although a majority of questions are on the nineteenth and twentieth centuries.

	Time Period	Approximate # of Questions
20%	Pre – Colonial to 1789	16
45%	1790 – 1914	36
35%	1915 to the present	28

Topics of Question on the test	Approximate percentage of questions on the test
Political institutions, behavior, and public policy	35%
Social and cultural developments	40%
Diplomacy and international relations	15%
Economic developments	10%

The multiple choice portion of the test counts for 50% of the exam grade and the essays portion as the other 50%. Within the essays section, the DBQ counts for 45 percent; the two standard essays together count for 55 percent.

Election and Presidential Term Years and Lame Ducks

A note about Presidential term years: Election years are always on even numbered years, every four years, and coincide with the decade every 20 years. So, for example, there were elections in 1800, 1804, 1808, 1816, 1820, 1840, 1860, etc. and there will be in 2020, 2040, 2060 and so on, with subsequent elections every 4 years in between. These elections take place in November of those years. However, the President does not take office until March (after the 20th amendment was adopted in 1933 it was moved to January) of the next year. For example, Dwight Eisenhower was elected in Nov. 1952, but took office in January of 1953. He served two terms and finished his Presidency in January, 1961 after JFK won the Presidency in November of 1960. So, technically his Presidency in office was from 1953 to 1961. However, I find it much easier to remember the Presidents by their election years since they occur on the even numbers, rather than actual years in office (odd years). For example,

Thomas Jefferson	1800 – 1808 (instead of 1801 – 1809)
James Madison	1808 – 1816 (instead of 1809 – 1817)
James Monroe	1816 – 1824 (instead of 1817 – 1825)

Therefore, I use this convention throughout this study guide. Just be aware that it is to help you remember the elections, but it is not strictly accurate as to their term in office.

Lastly, if a President is voted out of office or if they face term limits and cannot be elected again, during that period from the November election to the next term in March (January, after the 20th amendment) they are known as a "Lame Duck" President. It represents the unique period in which they are still President but the next President has been elected but not taken office yet. Often it is a time when not much can get done because Congress wants to wait until the new incoming President starts to enact any major legislation. However, it is also unique in that the President does not have to worry about the political consequences of their actions as much as usual. Because of this, they can make unpopular or potentially controversial decisions without having to worry if it will affect their reelection chances (they're on the way out anyway!).

Essay Writing Tips and Examples

Disclaimer: The following examples and tips do not guarantee any particular score and are simply the author's personal advice on what makes for good writing.

Several important things to keep in mind while writing essays for APUSH are:
1. Read the question carefully and make sure you understand what it's asking of you. Often there are several components to an essay and you want to make sure you are answering the right question. If a prompt asks you to discuss the reasons for colonial success in the Revolutionary War and you spend most of the essay discussing the various Acts that led up to the war then you have missed the question and are going to receive a very low score for failing to answer the correct question. I mention this because I have seen students do it numerous times. Sometimes the prompts can be complex and multi-faceted. For example, a prompt may ask you to examine the goals and outcomes for both whites and free blacks in the South during the pre - Civil War era. There are four parts you are expected to discuss in this essay (goals/outcomes for white/free blacks and it is limited to the South). Students often miss this and discuss only the goals or only the outcomes or not fully address those for either group. Don't stray out of the limits of the question.
2. Brainstorm for facts. Be sure to stick within the time parameters (if given). Spend a couple of minutes before writing your essay and list as many facts and details you can think of that might relate to the essay prompt. You may not end up using them all but it's good to start out with as much as possible. Remember: lots of outside information is important. You are demonstrating to the reader that you actually know a lot about the facts of U.S. history and can write about it in a clear, convincing manner.
3. Be sure to provide analysis (description, explanation, and tying ideas and points together)
4. Essay topics may include comparisons over time such as comparing immigrant experiences from different eras, or leaders of various movements (e.g. women's rights or the Civil Rights Era) from one time period to another.

Let's take a look at a sample prompt: Analyze the effects of the Industrial Revolution on immigrant populations and the spread of slavery for the period 1820 – 1850.

This essay might initially appear easy if you look only at the two qualifying topics: immigrant populations 1820 – 1850, Germans and the Irish, and the spread of slavery, from the Missouri Compromise (1820) to the Compromise of 1850. Boom, this looks easy. Just talk about these two topics. However, of course, the prompt is more specific, adding the limiting factor of the effects of the Industrial Revolution. Students are sometimes tempted by the wide openness of the two secondary topics and merely relegate mention of the Industrial Revolution to a statement such as: The Industrial Revolution had a major effect on immigrants while slavery spread dramatically up to 1850. They then proceed to provide lots of details about the immigrants and compromises of the time period, while failing to really answer the question of the effects of the Industrial Revolution. This must be avoided at all costs, because as said before, if you don't answer the question accurately, no matter how many facts you use, if they're answering the wrong question, it's wrong and you'll receive a low score.

<u>Specific Writing Advice and errors to avoid</u>

    1. Avoid I, we, you, us, our, or any other personal pronouns

    2. Avoid lessons in history – "… this is what made our country what it is today…", "slavery taught us…", "that's why America is great…" type of conclusions

    3. Use past tense – it's a history essay

    4. Avoid over-generalizing – "Everyone…," "All the colonies…," "All Americans were…"

    5. Don't speculate or guess; instead only make statements you are confident about and use facts to prove your points

    6. Avoid terms like "tons of," "huge," "it was totally" – they are too conversational

    7. Don't include moral judgments; E.g., an essay about slavery is probably not asking you if slavery was bad, but rather what led to its growth, etc. We all already agree that slavery was bad (hopefully!) so that's irrelevant.

<u>Good words/phrases to use</u>

To provide more info or elaborate: In addition, for example, furthermore

To compare or analyze: however, despite, although

To conclude (not just a conclusion paragraph, but to complete an idea or thought): thus, therefore, in the end, hence

<u>2 Sample prompts and responses</u>

1. Analyze the causes for the establishment of slavery in the colonies up to 1754.

    It was just twelve years after the 1607 founding of Jamestown in Virginia that the first 20 documented slaves were brought to the British colonies by Dutch traders. Despite this early introduction, slavery was not well established in the colonies in the early part of the 17th century. Only after a number of decades did slavery eventually became a mainstay, particularly in the southern colonies, because of the development of the plantation system, the preference of the usefulness of slaves over indentured servants, and the gradual affordability and availability of African slaves.

    In the early 1600s, slavery was not very common as slaves tended to be expensive and with widespread disease prevalent, they died too easily to be cost effective. More commonly used were cheaply acquired indentured servants who worked for several years to pay off their passage to the New World. Furthermore, under the "headright system," wealthy planters got 50 acres for every indentured servant for whose passage they paid. Therefore, the rich tended to get richer and more importantly, the early landowners increased their land holdings and set the stage for the plantation system. These plantations required many workers thus necessitating the import of a large labor force.

    With the growing need for many workers, the transition from the use of indentured servants to slaves included a number of factors. In South Carolina, in particular, slavery proved to have advantages over the use of indentured servants. The principle crop there was rice which many slaves already had previous experience cultivating before their bondage. In addition, many African slaves had a greater resistance to malaria compared to American Indians or indentured servants making them less likely to die in these situations. Of any singular event, however, it was Bacon's rebellion that led to the increased use of slaves. In 1676, Nathaniel Bacon led an uprising of disgruntled indentured servants in Virginia. Many were finding that upon gaining their freedom, there was only marginal land available and because it was on the frontiers, they were the first to be subject to Indian attacks. They succeeded in burning Jamestown and forcing Governor Berkeley to flee. In the end, the rebellion was quelled but not without causing the wealthy planters to distrust indentured servants. As a result, they began to see African slaves as a more manageable labor force. Unlike indentured servants, African slaves forcibly taken far from home, often not speaking the language, and with little hope of integrating far into society, were less able or likely to rebel or grumble against perceived lack of opportunities. Lastly, it became much easier and acceptable to enforce harsh slave codes and laws on Africans than fellow Europeans which allowed the assembly of a much larger force.

The final factor in the increase of using slaves was the affordability and availability of African slaves over indentured servants. By 1700, the Royal African Company had lost its monopoly for importing slaves, meaning no longer was there only one approved company for acquiring slaves. The result was many colonists, particularly New Englanders with ships, rushed to cash in on the slave trade, thus making slaves cheaper as well as an essential part of the Triangle Trade System. In addition, wages gradually rose in England during the late 1600s which reduced the number of indentured servants immigrating to the colonies.

The time from the early English colonies to the French and Indian War was a time of gradual increase in the use of slaves. Due to competition with indentured servitude, slavery as a system took some time to become firmly established there. However, due to the eventual needs for vast workers in the developing plantations, and the particular advantages and eventual cost-effectiveness African slaves had over indentured servants, slavery became a defining feature of labor in the colonial era.

2. Analyze the challenges faced by and solutions proposed for TWO of the following groups during the years 1865 – 1900.

    Industrial Workers   Immigrants   American Indians

Notice the two qualifying parts of the question: "challenges faced by" and "solutions proposed for." Don't miss this. Don't only talk about the various challenges; you need to be sure to address the solutions too.

The Gilded Age was a remarkable period of tremendous economic growth for the United States as the nation put the horrors of the Civil War behind it. Skyscrapers and railroads demonstrated the boom in business and production. However, despite this boom, there were many who confronted tremendous difficulties and took steps to overcome them. Countless workers in factories were taken advantage of by the their employers often leading to strikes or joining labor unions and American Indians were increasingly displaced on the Great Plains despite peaceful and violent resistance.

Much of the unprecedented amount of expansion occurring in the late 1800s was in the area of factory work and unskilled labor. Since such workers could easily be replaced and there was usually a surplus of workers, the result was generally low wages. In addition, because of the laissez faire attitude of the government, business was rarely regulated leading many big business owners to use harsh and manipulative practices to fuel their fortunes. Thus workers were often forced to work long hours, in poor working conditions, for miserable pay. Workers would sometimes be forced to sign yellow dog contracts, or iron-clad oaths, in which they'd be forced to agree not to join a union in order to be hired. Furthermore, workers often lived in company towns where the company controlled their housing and stores where they shopped.

In response to these difficult circumstances, the most common solution for workers was to get organized and join a union if they could. Two of the most recognized unions of the time were the Knights of Labor and the American Federation of Labor. The Knights were headed by Terrence Powderly and were advocating on behalf of workers everywhere, very much trying to overturn society as a whole, creating a much more balanced world. The AFL, however, led by Samuel Gompers, were more worried about solving the tangible problems of everyday workers: raising wages, shortening hours, and improving conditions. The AFL was a union made up of collections of skilled workers, which meant it had a stronger bargaining position as these types of workers are harder to replace. The Knights of Labor, on the other hand, allowed both skilled and unskilled laborers, creating a weakness in its efficiency and ability to create change. In the end, the Knights of Labor were associated with the notorious events of the Haymarket Riot resulting in their eventual unpopularity. The AFL and other smaller unions were more successful and long lasting, using their strength of numbers in strikes to gradually make some progress and small but significant improvements for workers. However, episodes such as the Homestead Strike and Pullman strike, with the government siding on the side of the business owners, is evidence that organized labor was often not successful in its efforts to dramatically solve the challenges they faced during the Gilded Age.

The late nineteenth century represented the last major era of American Indian conflicts. By this point, many of the free tribes lived upon the Great Plains where they depended on the vast buffalo herds. With white settlements encroaching upon their tribal areas, Native Americans were gradually forced onto marginal reservation land. In an attempt to break the spirit and way of life of the Plains Indians, buffalo were systematically destroyed to near extinction. Some natives resisted and fought the U.S. army, scoring the occasional victory such as at Little Bighorn, in which Colonel Custer and his men were wiped out. However, more often than not, the American Indians were forced to capitulate. Even when attempting to use peaceful means, as did the Cheyenne under Black Kettle and White Antelope, were they often betrayed and attacked. Despite receiving promises by President Lincoln of peace if they cooperated, many of them were killed in the Sand Creek Massacre of 1864. To further inhibit the ability of Native Americans to wage war, Indian children were often taken from their parents and forced to assimilate in western style schools, learning western culture. In 1887, Congress passed the Dawes Act which broke up reservations into individually family owned parcels, hoping to encourage them to settle down and become more like white farmers. As a result of all this, American Indians were ultimately not very successful at overcoming the daunting challenge they faced. The last tragedy of the era came at Wounded Knee when U.S. soldiers opened fire on unarmed men, women, and children, massacring more than a hundred.

Overall, the Gilded Age proved to be an overwhelming time for many who weren't members of the elite wealthy class. Workers faced harsh conditions in dismal factories, with unsympathetic employers and little government protections. Despite this, workers often united in labor unions and were successful in gaining some modest improvements. American Indians, on the other hand, were less successful during this time period, being forced onto reservations throughout. Despite violent and nonviolent resistance, westward expansion inevitably crushed their efforts and closed the frontier.

Keep in mind, these samples are meant to be examples of the sorts of things that should be included and the approach and style that is appropriate. For many students, it may be a challenge to include so many details in the short space of a timed writing test, while keeping the essay organized and focused on answering the question. I would encourage you to see these as models of style, to study the facts in the review, and practice brainstorming for each era so you have a lot of facts at your disposal to answer the wide possibilities of questions that may be asked.

1. Colonial Era

A. Pre – Colonial and other important details

- Europeans improved maritime technology, began to develop large nation-states which could finance exploration, and developed more advanced weapons allowing them to explore and conquer the New World
- Spain – The *Reconquista* – Spain pushed out the Muslim Moors from Spain to unite the country under Ferdinand and Isabella. They funded Columbus's voyage to the New World in 1492. He thought he had reached India thus calling the natives "Indians."
- Treaty of Tordesillas (1494) – Spain and Portugal draw a line dividing up the New World; Spain gets everything west, Portugal the east (turned out to be basically Brazil)
- Columbian Exchange – the swapping of plants, animals, diseases, ideas from the Old World and New World (E.g. Native Americans didn't have horses but the introduction of them by Euros transformed the Great Plains tribes making them much more mobile, etc.)
- See Native American History section for more of early history

B. Spanish

- *Conquistadores* took over large parts of South and Central America – God, Glory, and Gold
- Setup *encomiendas* – system of using natives for slave labor (searching for gold; farming, etc)
- The "Black Legend" – the myth that the Spanish were the worst of the European colonizers. Despite the aggressiveness and harshness of the conquistadores, many Spanish settlers tended to interact more with the native peoples than the English. Catholic priests set up many missions and attempted to convert the natives. They also tended to intermarry much more with the native population creating a mixed heritage people/culture. Contrast this with the view of many English who saw the natives as disposable.
- Bartolome de las Casas – a Spanish priest who criticized Spanish treatment of the natives
- Pueblo Revolt (a.k.a. Pope's Rebellion) (1680)
    - Natives in the Southwest rebel against the Spanish and succeed in destroying churches and pushing the Spanish out for about 10 years. Then Pope, the leader, dies and the Spanish return.

Quick interlude – It's worth talking a bit about religion here…

The Spanish and French were overwhelmingly Catholic; the English were mostly Protestant…what's the deal?

Both are Christian but they disagree on some fundamental things that traditionally caused lots of tension, leading even to wars and killings of each other. Catholics believe in a level of divinity of Mary, confess to priests, and submit authority to the Pope. Protestants, who "protested" originally under Martin Luther, rejected many of these ideas and thought it was more "authentic" to have a more direct relationship with God.

What they both had in common was usually that they felt that God had led them to the New World, that the natives were heathens/pagans (non-believers, thus less worthy), and that they had the right to forcibly occupy and utilize the New World.

C. French

- Settled primarily in Canada (Quebec); explored and claimed land along the Mississippi
- Low numbers of settlers; mostly fur trappers hunting beavers

- As a result, they tended to work *with* Indians rather than displace them

D. Southern English Colonies
- Characteristics: Good climate and soil for growing. In the early years tended to be many young, single men, especially in the settlement of the Chesapeake colonies (Virginia, Maryland). Although religion was important, southern colonists were more economically motivated.
- Virginia
  - Started by the Virginia Company, a joint stock company where investors finance the venture but expect profits to be returned; thus the VA colony was motivated by finding/making money
  - Jamestown (1607) – disease ridden as it was built near a swamp
  - John Smith – work or don't eat; leaves in 1608
  - Starving time (1609-10) – colony nearly extinct but a relief ship arrived
  - Tobacco – introduced by John Rolfe in 1612
  - Tobacco was very profitable early on ("poor man's crop") but it ruins the soil; thus more and more land is needed; this expansion naturally leads to conflicts with natives (see Bacon's Rebellion below)
  - 1619 – 1st 20 slaves arrive; House of Burgesses (representative gov't) established
  - In the early years most workers were indentured servants – someone who pays for their passage to the New World in exchange for several years of service
  - The death rate in VA in the early years was high because of disease, Indian attacks, etc. Population growth was only by immigration; not enough births.
  - Because women were scarce, they tended to have more rights than women in New England
  - Anglo-Powhatan Wars – conflicts with local Indians (Pocahontas's tribe)
  - Headright System – to encourage population growth, anyone who paid for an indentured servant's passage to the New World got 50 acres…this allowed for rich individuals to get huge amounts of land leading to the eventual plantation system (which helped fuel slavery in the South)
  - Bacon's Rebellion (1676) – frustration of poor indentured servants who upon gaining their freedom found that most of the good land was taken; the only available land was on the frontier, but that led to increasing Indian attacks; Nathanial Bacon led a rebellion against the planter class, burning Jamestown as a result and forcing the governor (Berkeley) to flee. Bacon died of disease and the rebellion collapsed but the result was less use of indentured servants and an increased use of slaves (major turning point in the history of slavery).
  - See African American History for more specifics about the early history of colonial slavery
- Maryland
  - Refuge for Catholics; Lord Baltimore
  - Like Virginia, tobacco/indentured servants were also a major part of Maryland
  - Act of Toleration (1649) – passed to protect Catholics who were gradually being outnumbered by Protestants (otherwise, it was not very tolerant!)
  - Maryland and Virginia together known as the Chesapeake colonies because of the bay nearby
- S. Carolina
  - Principal crop was rice. Rice production is very labor intensive. Africans were skilled in rice cultivation so many were brought to S. Carolina.

- - - Eventually it had a majority slave population (also making S.C. more supportive of slavery)
    - Imported the slave codes from Barbados to deal with increasing numbers of slaves
  - N. Carolina
    - Less aristocratic than neighbors S. Carolina/Virginia; more independent
  - Georgia
    - Founded as a "buffer state" between Spanish and French and the more valuable colonies like S. Carolina
    - James Oglethorpe was one of the early founders; wanted to create a haven for people in debtors' prison

Triangle Trade – trade between Europe (manufactured goods) to Africa (slaves) to the New World (raw materials) and back to Europe

Middle Passage – the leg of the journey from Africa to the Americas in which slaves were transported. Conditions were harsh and crowded, with disease and starvation claiming many lives before even arriving in the New World.

E. West Indies
- Sugar was the primary crop (a "rich man's crop" because it was expensive to produce)
- Required many slaves (that's why places like Haiti, etc. have large black populations)

F. Middle English Colonies
- Characteristics: Most diverse; lots of different European groups; breadbasket colonies
- New Jersey
- Delaware – originally New Sweden
- Pennsylvania
  - Founded by William Penn as a refuge for Quakers (a "Holy Experiment")
  - Quakers believed anybody could be saved (spiritually); were abolitionists, pacifists, refused to take oaths and had good relations with Indians; thus, they were persecuted
- New York – New York City – originally New Amsterdam

G. New England English Colonies
- Characteristics: Soil tended to be poor and rocky in many areas, therefore subsistence agriculture was widespread. Shipbuilding, lumber, fishing, commerce were increasingly common. Religion was very important, e.g. the Pilgrims and Puritans. In the early years, they tended to come to America in family groups. Much healthier climate than the southern colonies.
- Massachusetts
  - Pilgrims (1620) – first settled at Plymouth. They were Separatists who wanted to split from the Church of England. Formed the Mayflower Compact, an agreement to form a political body in the New World. Led by William Bradford.
    - Eventually Plymouth was absorbed by the Mass. Bay Colony
  - Puritans (1630) – Massachusetts Bay Colony – Puritans were also frustrated with the English (Anglican) church but they didn't want to separate from it; they wanted to "purify" the church from within

- Great Migration (1630s) – many Puritans came to New England.
- They wanted to create a model godly society; one of the early governors, John Winthrop said they should be like "a city upon a hill." Because of this, the colonial gov't and the church were closely related (gov't is enforcing God's laws, so to disobey the colonial gov't was to disobey God!).
- They believed in predestination – the idea that it has already been decided if you're going to heaven or not. Therefore, Puritans tended to value hard work as it was a sign that you were chosen (known as the Puritan work ethic).
- Roger Williams – believed in separation of church and state (scandalous to the Puritans!) and that they should pay the Indians for their land (those heathens don't deserve our money!...or so they may have thought)
- Anne Hutchinson – she supported antinomianism, or the belief that if predestination is true, then you don't need to follow gov't laws (uh, no way was that going to fly with the Puritans)
- Both Williams and Hutchinson were banished
- To promote marriage and family values, women tended to give up or lose many rights to create dependency and attempt to keep families together
- Pequot War (1636) – English colonists massacre natives
- King Philip's War (1676) – natives attack villages along the frontier; massacre many settlers. However, the next year the English settlers attack and push the natives further back (Lesson: native rebellions rarely work).
- 1693 – Salem Witch Trials – a classic example of the church going too far
- Rhode Island
  - Allowed freedom of religion
  - Where Roger Williams settled; where other Puritan "rejects" went
- Connecticut, New Hampshire
  - More Puritan settlements
  - In Connecticut, they wrote the *Fundamental Orders of Connecticut,* a set of written laws for the colony. It's the first example of a Constitution in the New World.
- Half-way covenant – by mid 1600s church membership was declining so this gave people partial membership in the church (kept people in the church by watering down the requirements) – no longer the "city upon a hill"
- Town hall meetings were important in New England. Tradition of talking over issues at the town hall.
- Education was important; children needed to be able to read the Bible

H. Miscellaneous Colonial details
- Tax supported churches: (so government and religion mixed)
  - Church of England (Anglican) mostly in the southern colonies
  - Congregational Church mostly dominant in New England (Puritan)
- The Great Awakening (1730s – 1740s)
  - After a few generations of settlers, many of the Puritan descendants were not so passionate about religion as their forefathers. Therefore the Great Awakening was a spiritual revival intended to "awaken" people to take religion more seriously.
  - More focused on spiritual rebirth and emotions than previous generations

o Jonathan Edwards – Sinners in the Hands of an Angry God – most famous sermon
- Trial of John Peter Zenger
  o JPZ was sued because he wrote criticisms of a local politician
  o Because the criticisms were true, he was not found guilty
  o Important because it helped establish an early tradition of freedom of press

2. The French and Indian and Revolutionary Wars

A. French and Indian War
- 1754-1763 in America
- 1756-1763 in Europe (hence, known there as the 'Seven Years War')
- Fought between France and Britain and their Indian allies
- Washington, as a surveyor at the time, started the conflict when he attacked some French in the Ohio valley; he was defeated at Fort Necessity but allowed to leave
- 1754 – Albany Plan – discussion over whether Iroquois would remain loyal to the British; Ben Franklin's famous 'Join or Die' cartoon; early call to colonial unity
- 1759 – Battle of Quebec – Britain wins; major defeat of the French
- 1763 – The Treaty of Paris ends the war with France, who essentially lose their lands, while Britain becomes the undisputed master of North America
- Aftermath: Without the common enemy of France, and Britain racking up a large war debt, tensions increase between Britain and the colonies, with Britain expecting the colonies to pay up for its defenses. Thus Britain ends salutary neglect (see below).
- Pontiacs Rebellion in 1763 – Native Am. leader Pontiac unites tribes in the Ohio valley and attacks Ft. Detroit and attempts to push American colonists back east. The result is:
- Proclamation of 1763 – with the British fearing greater war debts defending the colonists from Indians, they prohibit the colonists from settling west of the Appalachians. Colonists feel this is betrayal of the sacrifices of the war and pour west anyway. Tensions rise!

B. Relationship between England and the colonies
- Mercantilism
  o The colonies provide raw materials (lumber, tobacco, etc.) to the England (mother country), while England produces manufactured goods (tools, clothes, etc.) which the colonies are the market for. I.e., colonies are subservient to and exist to make profit for the mother country
- Navigation Laws (1650) – Essentially required the colonies to trade only with G.B.
- Salutary neglect – "beneficial neglect" – Great Britain would turn a blind eye to some of the colonies smuggling and disobedience of the Navigation Laws, as long as they were compliant and the economy was good. Under this, the enforcement of the Navigation Laws was weak (key idea: after the French/Indian War, salutary neglect ends).

C. Leadup to the Revolutionary War
- Britain was in debt after the French/Indian War so they expected the colonists to pay their share since the war was at least partially fought for their defense. The colonists were not opposed to paying taxes but felt that "taxation without representation" was unfair.
  o The British argued that colonists had "virtual representation," that is, that Parliament had the colonies best interest at heart and represented them fairly
- 1764 – Sugar Act

- 1765 – Quartering Act – colonists required to house soldiers in their homes, taverns, etc.
- 1765 – Stamp Act – tax on paper products; you had to buy the stamp even to buy playing cards…
    - Violators tried in courts with no trial by jury
    - Colonial reactions included: tarring/feathering officials, non-importation agreements (limited boycotts), formation of the Sons/Daughters of Liberty
    - Stamp Act Congress formed to express colonial grievances
    - Eventually repealed because boycotts were hurting British companies; hmmm, victory for colonists? This colonial unity thing might work out!
- 1767 – Townshend Acts (taxes on variety – glass, lead, paint, etc).
    - Failure of colonists to follow the Acts leads to troops in Boston
    - Leads to Boston Massacre in 1770 (colonists provoke the redcoats)
- 1772 – Committees of Correspondence formed (Samuel Adams) to organize resistance and spread propaganda between colonies
- 1774 – Tea monopoly granted to British company resulting in the Boston Tea Party
    - Coercive (Intolerable) Acts passed to get Bostonians to follow the law
        - Includes closing Boston Port and the Quebec Act (favorable to French)
- 1774 – First Continental Congress meets – grievances sent to the king; complete boycott of British goods declared
- 1775 – Patrick Henry: "Give me liberty or give me death!"
- 1775 – Battles of Lexington and Concord begin the war ("Shot heard round the world")

D. The Revolutionary War
- 1775 – 2nd Continental Congress meets to make decisions about the war effort
    - Issued the Olive Branch Petition – a last desperate attempt to make peace with king George III
- *Common Sense* by Thomas Paine – argued reasons for independence
- Declaration of Independence (1776) by Thomas Jefferson
    - "All men are created equal"; expresses inalienable rights
    - Lists all the grievances the colonists had against King George III
    - Original draft condemned the British for promoting slavery but southern delegates didn't like any negative views of slavery so it was removed
- Loyalists/Tories – colonists who were loyal to the British; rebellious colonists = Patriots
- Hessians – German mercenaries hired by the British
- Battle of Trenton (1776) – Washington (Commander of the Continental Army) crosses the Delaware river on Christmas night and captures ~ 1,000 Hessians
- Valley Forge – location of the Continental Army in 1777-78, during which they suffered from considerable shortages and the cold winter
- Battle of Saratoga (1777) – convinces France to join on the side of the Patriots which was key to American victory (they needed supplies, naval support, loans, etc.)
- Battle of Yorktown (1781) – last major battle of the war; Cornwallis surrenders after being surrounded by the French at sea and the colonials by land
- Treaty of Paris (1783) officially ends the war

3. The Critical Period and first six Presidents

- Slavery began being abolished in the northern states, but the south held onto it. After a war fought "for freedom and rights," the new country was in an awkward position of being against slavery ideals but the South being economically dependent upon it.
- Women also sought more power and responsibility
  - Republican Motherhood – women's responsibility to raise virtuous children who would continue the legacy of republican values (loyalty, honesty, freedom, etc.)
- 1781 – The Articles of Confederation (AoC) created
  - 1st government of the U.S. It lasts until 1787
  - Approved only after large states gave up their claims to western lands; this land will then be administered by the national government
  - Designed to be a weak central gov't opposite of the recent monarch/strong central government (so the below weaknesses were not perceived to be weak initially, but rather essential and desirable)
- Weaknesses of the AoC:
  - No power to tax; could only ask states to volunteer to pay
  - Could not regulate commerce (foreign and domestic)
  - No Executive (President) branch because of fear of a king figure
  - Equal representation (1 vote) in Congress (gave small states as much power as big states)
  - 2/3 majority (9 of 13 states) needed to pass legislation
  - Required unanimous (all 13) vote to amend the Articles (thus, hard to change!)
  - States had most of the power, therefore, the central/national gov't under the Articles could not force states to do almost anything. The result was disunity and chaos.

- Successes of the AoC:
  - Negotiated the end of the Revolutionary War
  - Kept the United States together during this critical period, if even just loosely
  - Land Ordinance of 1785
    - Established that the sale of public lands (now owned by the national gov't) would be used to pay off national debts
  - Northwest Ordinance of 1787
    - Forbade slavery in Northwest; established 60,000 as the threshold for new statehood; important because now there is a peaceful standard for state admission rather than old states battling out for more territory

- Shays' Rebellion (1786) – Daniel Shays leads a rebellion of farmers (who were in debt) in Massachusetts against the gov't. It is nearly successful as the U.S. gov't is so weak it can't put the rebellion down. Ultimately it is put down by a private state militia.
  - Importance: Shows the weakness of the AoC; that it can't handle such a rebellion; major impetus (driving force) for its revision and replacement.
- Constitutional Convention (in Philadelphia) and resulting Constitution: (1787)
  - Were supposed to revise the AoC – decided to scrap them and start over
  - Created a republic or representative democracy: one in which the people elect representatives to represent them in gov't as opposed to a direct democracy
  - Federal system (federalism): balance between national and state gov'ts
  - Separation of branches:

- Legislative: creates the laws (Congress)
- Executive: enforces the laws (President and Departments [e.g. of state])
- Judicial: interprets the laws (Supreme Ct.)
  - Great Compromise: To satisfy both large and small states, Congress is made up of two parts: (known as a bicameral [or two body] legislature)
    - House of Representatives (representation is based on population)
    - Senate (representation is equal; 2 per state)
  - 3/5 Compromise: In determining representation based on population, slaves counted as 3/5 of a person; Note: this does NOT mean that slaves could vote and their vote counted as 3/5 of a vote. Slaves could NOT vote. Since representation in the House of Representatives meant power in the national gov't, having more reps meant more power. Therefore, the South wanted their slaves to count so they'd have more reps, but the North thought they shouldn't count at all since they were not treated as citizens. Hence the dastardly compromise of fractioning a person. In addition, as part of this, the slave <u>trade</u> was to not be abolished until 1807. When this date came, Congress did indeed ban bringing new slaves to the U.S. Both of these compromises highlight the delicate nature of slavery and the desire to keep the fragile Union together rather than risk tearing it at the outset.
  - Checks and balances: each branch has some power to limit the others. E.g. the Pres. can veto legislation, but Congress can vote to impeach the President…
  - A balance: not so much freedom of the people/masses that "mobocracy" might occur, but not too much gov't power to prevent tyranny
  - Congress has the power to tax, regulate commerce, etc. all the things the AoC couldn't do basically
- Ratification
  - Anti – federalists opposed the Constitution
    - Feared too much power in the gov't (tyranny)
    - Demanded a Bill of Rights to guarantee freedoms
  - Federalists supported the Constitution
  - Federalists Papers – written by John Jay, Alexander Hamilton, and James Madison – a series of arguments FOR the ratification of the Constitution
  - Bill of Rights approved in 1789 (in effect by 1791) – First 10 amendments

<u>George Washington (1789 – 1796) (no party affiliation)</u>
- Hamilton believed a national debt was a good thing because then people to whom the gov't owed money wanted to see this new Republican experiment succeed!
- Hamilton got the national gov't to <u>assume</u>, or take on, the states' debts (Assumption)
- To achieve the above two, Hamilton created a Bank of the United States
- Loose vs. strict constructionist (interpretation) view of the Constitution
  - Strict (literal, narrow, limited) interpretation = federal gov't only has powers that are explicitly written in the Constitution; if it's not said, it can't be done by the federal gov't
  - Loose (broad, wide, loosey-goosey) interpretation = it is implied that the federal gov't can do certain things, even if the Constitution doesn't say it specifically. Based on the "elastic clause" that says Congress can do whatever is "necessary and proper" to fulfill its specifically listed duties (Article 1, Section 8, Clause 18)
    - The classic example of this was the debate over creating the 1st Bank of the U.S. Hamilton wanted to create it but Jefferson said the Constitution didn't grant it. However, said Hamilton, if a bank is "necessary" in order

for Congress to fulfill its other powers (e.g., coin money and regulate commerce), then creating a bank is allowed. Scandalous stuff!

- Whiskey Rebellion (1794) – farmers rebelling against a whiskey tax. Unlike Shays' rebellion, this rebellion is successfully put down by Hamilton and Washington.
  - Importance: it demonstrates and confirms the strength of the new power of the federal gov't under the Constitution

Early development of parties (despite Washington warning against them)

Federalists	Democratic Republicans (former anti-feds)
Hamilton	Jefferson
Favored strong central gov't	Favored more power in the states
Loose construction	Strict construction
Pro-British	Pro-French
Favored cities, commercial class, Northeast	Favored farmers, South, rural

- Washington's Neutrality Proclamation (1793) – throughout the first few presidencies, Britain and France were often at war. Washington decided America was too weak to take a side in this latest mid 1790s conflict.
- Genet Affair – a Frenchman, Genet, came to America and tried to raise an army among the people to support France but it failed. The people listened to their President!
- Jay's Treaty (1795) – essentially gave Britain most of what it wanted. Seen by many in America as a sell out to Britain.
- Farewell Address
  - Warned of permanent alliances and political parties
  - Set a precedent by willingly giving up power after two terms (what a guy!)

John Adams (1796 – 1800) (Federalist)
- Incidents with France as a result of the U.S. not helping them against the British
  - XYZ Affair – 3 French diplomats (XYZ) demand a bribe from American officials
  - Quasi – War – a pseudo, undeclared war with France – mostly fighting on the seas
- Alien and Sedition Acts passed (1798) to silence/hinder the Federalist critics
  - Alien Act – gave the federal gov't greater power to deport immigrants and changed citizenship requirement from 5 to 14 years (many immigrants were aligned with the Democratic-Republicans, so this was a method of disenfranchising many of them to enable the Feds to win elections)
  - Sedition Act – fines or imprisonment for anyone speaking "bad" about the government, specifically about the Federalists (sedition, in general, means speaking or organizing against the gov't, usually in a rebellious manner)
- Kentucky/Virginia (KY/VA) Resolutions – Hello!?!, weren't these Alien/Sedition Acts violating basic rights (the anti-feds were right; fear a strong central gov't!)? Therefore, KY and VA said they "nullified" the laws; that is, they did not recognize the power of the federal gov't to pass such laws and declared their states would not allow them.
  - Importance: the battle between states and federal gov't is already heating up and we're only at our 2nd President! Who has more power, the states or the central gov't? Taken to its extreme, this will later be the basis for further nullification and ultimately secession.

<u>Thomas Jefferson (1800-1808) (Democratic Republican)</u>

- 1800 – Jefferson is elected over John Adams – the anti-federalists (now Democratic-Republicans) take power from the Federalists. The result is a "revolutionary" election – a peaceful transition of power!

- 1803 – 2 Important Events
  - Louisiana Purchase – the U.S. paid $15 million to France/Napoleon. Effectively doubles the size of the U.S. at the time. Jefferson was reluctant because it wasn't clear if it was legal under the Constitution (and he's a strict interpreter), however, it was ultimately too good to pass up. Lewis and Clark are then sent to explore and map out the area.
  - *Marbury v. Madison* – <u>Chief Justice John Marshall</u> decides in favor of Madison, overturning the Judiciary Act of 1789; the result is that the Supreme Court decides the constitutionality of that law. This increased the power of the Judicial branch. It established the idea of <u>judicial review</u> – <u>the idea that the Supreme Court can determine whether a law is constitutional or not.</u> When I say *Marbury v. Madison,* you say…?

- 1807 – Embargo Act – England and France were once again at war and attempting to force America's involvement, therefore, Jefferson issued an embargo, not allowing America to trade with either country. The result was that America suffered the most with the loss of trade; O Grab Me! (Embargo backwards). Hugely unpopular. Madison cancels it the next year when he is President.

<u>James Madison (1808 – 1816) (Democratic Republican)</u>
War of 1812 – A second war for independence?
- Causes:
  - Impressment: The British were forcing American sailors to serve in their navy
  - British arming Nat. Americans in the frontier lands against American colonists
  - Chesapeake incident (1807): The Chesapeake was a ship that the British attacked in order to capture deserters. The U.S. was not at war with Britain so this was rather scandalous!
  - War hawks – people who clamor (demand) for war; in this case, many war hawks were Southerners who were anti-British
- Significant Events:
  - Bombardment at Fort McHenry (Baltimore); Francis Scott Key watched this and wrote the Star Spangled Banner
  - The British manage to attack and burn Washington D.C.
  - Treaty of Ghent – ended the war in December 1814. Ended without resolving any issues that caused the conflict; known as *status quo antebellum* (same as before the war).
  - Battle of New Orleans (Jan. 1815) – Andrew Jackson is the hero of this battle even though it happens technically after the war is over
- Effects:
  - A sense nationalism swept the country ("we didn't win the war…but we didn't lose it either! We're #1, we're #1…!" – not a direct quote by the way!)
  - Hartford Convention
    - New England Federalists opposed the war because it hurt their trade with England. They threatened to nullify laws and demanded changes in the

Constitution to prevent future wars. Contrasted to the air of nationalism elsewhere, this caused the decline of the Federalists.
- The American System – devised by Henry Clay, it was a plan to build up America and was a result of the post-war nationalism. 3 goals:
    1) Tariff of 1816 – tariff to protect Amer. companies from foreign competition (this benefited New England most and tended to hurt southern farmer states)
    2) A 2nd Bank of the U.S.
    3) Building roads/canals to improve the economy/transportation

James Monroe (1816 – 1824) (Democratic Republican)
- His Presidency is known as the "Era of Good Feelings" because there is essentially only one party in power at the time: the Democratic – Republicans. However, it was anything but "good" what with the Panic of 1819 and Missouri Compromise.
- Panic of 1819 – a downturn in the economy caused by banks giving out too much money and people speculating (buying to make profit, not to own) on western lands
- Adams-Onis Treaty (1819) – U.S. got Florida and gave up claims in TX to Spain (see expansion chart for more)
- Missouri Compromise (1820) – Missouri wanted statehood as a slave state, however, that would throw off the current equal balance (and power) of slave/free states. Therefore, Maine was added to the Union also as a free state. In addition, the Compromise forbade all other slavery above the line 36° 30″ within the Louisiana Purchase (note this did not limit future land acquisitions from Mexico north of 36° 30″). Delayed the slavery controversy.
- Monroe Doctrine (1823) – essentially stated that European powers should no longer try to colonize or interfere in the Western Hemisphere; stay out of our backyard, our hood, our crib

John Quincy Adams (1824 – 1828) ("Republican – Generic" – that is, no identifiable party)
- Election of 1824 – The "Corrupt Bargain"
    - Mainly between Andrew Jackson, J.Q. Adams, and Henry Clay
    - No candidate receives a majority of electoral votes (but Jackson got the most of the 4), so the decision is sent to the House of Representatives. Clay is the Speaker of the House so he arranges to have Adams win, and Adams makes Clay his secretary of state (scandalous!). Many felt Jackson should have won.
    - Jackson gets his revenge when he defeats Adams in the election of 1828 (in yo' face!).

4. The Jacksonian Era
Andrew Jackson (1828 – 1836) (Democrat)
- Self-made man; famous Indian fighter and hero of Battle of New Orleans
- Tough; known as "Old Hickory"
- Ushers in the "Era of the Common Man" – more people could vote as state property requirements were dropped; also known as Jacksonian Democracy
- Permanent establishment of the two-party system (Democrats vs. Whigs at the time)
- Uses the Spoils System (also a type of patronage) – help me get elected and I'll make sure you have a job in the gov't. More turnover in gov't is good because politicians who are in gov't for too long get out of touch with the people (according to Jackson). Every "common man" can fulfill gov't duties…

- Jackson used the veto power more than all Presidents before him combined
  - Maysville Road Veto – KY wanted to use federal funds to build an <u>intra</u>state (not crossing state lines) road. Congress (federal government) only controls <u>inter</u>state commerce, so Jackson argued the government was overstepping its bounds.
- Nullification Crisis
  - Starts with the enactment of the Tariff of Abominations in 1828 (remember, tariffs are taxes on foreign goods, thus a raise protects domestic manufactured goods. In this way, tariffs helped New England companies where lots of stuff was made but hurt the South who depended on buying lots of equipment, etc.)
  - S. Carolina threatened to nullify, or cancel, the tariff. Basically they weren't going to enforce it (or add the tariff on incoming imports) in S. Carolina (uh oh, a showdown is beginning!)
  - J. Calhoun (the V.P.!) anonymously writes the *South Carolina Exposition and Protest* in support of S. Carolina (Pres. vs. Vice Pres.) [Calhoun will soon resign.]
  - Jackson was not going to allow a state to threaten the Union or disobey the federal gov't, so Congress passed the Force Act, authorizing the Pres. to use military force to enforce the collection of the tariff (federal vs. state powers issue).
  - Henry Clay negotiates a compromise (1833) in which the tariff is reduced over 10 years
  - S. Carolina repeals nullification of the tariff (whew, an early Civil War averted!)
- 1830 – Congress passes the Indian Removal Act – forced natives from the Southeast (Georgia, Florida, etc.), including the "5 Civilized Tribes" to the west of the Mississippi (Oklahoma primarily)
- Bank War – Jackson saw the 2nd Bank of the U.S. as elitist and a tool of the eastern bankers against farmers in the West
  - Election of 1832 – Jackson vs. Clay – Clay used the issue of the Bank to try to get Jackson out of the Presidency. It backfired and Jackson used the popular anger against the bank to remove gov't funds from it and wait for its charter to expire, thus "killing" it.

<u>Martin Van Buren (1836 – 1840) (Democrat)</u>
- Trail of Tears – thousands of Cherokee are relocated to Oklahoma; 4,000 die on the way. A result of Jackson's Indian policy and 1830 Removal Act (see above).
- Panic of 1837 – downturn in the economy; decline of the Bank of U.S. and over speculation of western lands and gov't monetary policy all contributed to causes. Ruined Van Buren's Presidency.

<u>William Henry Harrison (1840) (Whig)</u>
- Harrison was an Indian fighting war hero (Battle of Tippecanoe); ran with John Tyler as VP, therefore their campaign slogan was "Tippecanoe and Tyler too!"
- Died 1 month into the office
- Log Cabin campaign – Although Harrison was a wealthy plantation owner, since Jackson earlier won the election as the "common man," it became a winning strategy to try to win votes by portraying yourself in a humble way (growing up in a log cabin)

5. Themes of the early-mid 19th century (1800s) (Industrial Revolution, Immigration, Reforms, Slavery)

A. Industrial Revolution

- Gradual increase in use of technology; increased patents for inventions, change from hand-made goods to mass produced factory-made goods
- Market Revolution (as part of this whole transition/revolution) – decline of subsistence agriculture; rise of wages for work; goods begin being mass produced in factories (not all, but the process begins, mostly in textiles [clothing])
- "Cult of domesticity" – idealized the role of women as homemakers; raise children
- Eli Whitney – interchangeable parts – enabled mass production and division of labor
- Conditions could be harsh; 12 – 14 hours, child labor, hazardous work conditions; women and children paid less and exploited
- Example of early factory: Lowell Mill in Massachusetts
  - Workers were often New England farm girls; eventually replaced by Irish women
  - Women were monitored/supervised while on and off work
- Transportation
  - Steamboats
    - Could travel upstream; cut down shipping times
    - Very popular in mid-1800s
  - Canals – man-made waterways to connect other bodies of water
    - Erie Canal – 1825 – connected Great Lakes (Chicago, Buffalo, etc.) to NY City and Atlantic. Reduced shipping costs for the Northwest/Great Lakes
  - Railroads 1830s – 1860s (first big initial growth)
    - Subsidized by federal gov't – mostly in the form of cash and land grants (millions of acres). Railroads, in turn, sold this land to developers/farmers for profit.
  - Communication
    - Telegraph – developed by Samuel Morse – instant communication
    - Pony Express – quick mail to West coast; 1860; lasted only 18 months
- Agriculture – development of steel plow, mechanical reaper – all allow for increased production, less hands needed, and more market agriculture (growing for profit)
- A result of all the above was the increasing specialization of each region since they could import what they didn't produce: the South grew cotton for export, the West grain and livestock to feed factory workers in the East and Europe, and the East made machines and textiles for the other regions

B. Immigration – the "Old Immigrants" (the first big wave) – English, Irish, and Germans

Irish	Germans
Came to America after the potato famine in the 1840s	Came to America after the failed revolution of 1848, fleeing autocratic rule; crop failures
Settled in the Northeast cities	After arriving, tended to move to the Midwest
Came over poor and unskilled	Tended to come with more wealth and education
Catholic	More often Protestant
Competition with blacks for jobs	Lived in tight knit communities
NINA – No Irish Need Apply	Alcohol
Alcohol	
Concentrated political power in the cities (political machines)	

- Nativism (nativist) – the movement against foreigners/immigrants
- Know Nothing Party – a.k.a., the Order of the Star Spangled Banner, a nativist political party in the mid 1800s

C. Antebellum Reform Movements
- Reform movements, in general, were something that tried to improve society in some way
- 2nd Great Awakening – a second religious revival (1820s – 1840s)
  - More emotional and focused on personal salvation than 1st G.A.
  - Camp meetings – widespread revival; very emotional
  - Women play a major role
  - Major cause or inspiration of subsequent reforms
  - Mormonism develops – Joseph Smith (founder); Brigham Young continues
  - Deism – belief in some sort of God force but universe operates on natural laws (not personal or organized religion)
- Prison and insane asylum reform – Dorothea Dix; place to rehabilitate instead of punish
- Education reform
  - Horace Mann: improve and expand public schools (including better teacher pay and training, less corporal punishment)
  - McGuffy Readers – new books that taught reading as well as morals; reinforced social hierarchy at times
- Temperance – movement to reduce/end drinking of alcohol
  - Alcohol seen as ruining many families; caused injuries in factories; "demon rum"
  - American Temperance Society (Founded 1826)
  - T.S. Arthur wrote a book called, "Ten Nights in a Barroom and What I Saw There" (1854) dramatizing the terrible effects of alcohol on a small town
  - Neil S. Dow, known as the "Father of Prohibition," helped pass the Maine Law (1851), the first state to prohibit sale and manufacture of alcohol
  - See Temperance/Prohibition for more, beyond this time period
- Women's rights
  - Seneca Falls Convention (1848): Leading women meet and draw up the Declaration of Sentiments ("…that all men and women are created equal…")
  - Susan B. Anthony, Elizabeth Cady Stanton, Lucy Stone, Elizabeth Blackwell
    - See Women's History for more…
- Utopian communities – attempts to create a "perfect" or "ideal" society
  - New Harmony – founded by Robert Owen – communal ownership of land
  - Oneida – by John Noyes – "complex marriage" i.e. free love; silverware maker
  - Brook Farm – Transcendentalist utopia; burned down after a fire
  - Shakers – Christian utopian group
- Transcendentalism
  - Belief in a truth that transcends normal senses
  - Rejected materialism and slavery; believed in self-reliance
  - Ralph Waldo Emerson
  - Henry David Thoreau
    - Live simply (book: Walden, living in the woods)
    - Book: Civil Disobedience – passive resistance (later affected MLK, Gandhi)
- Abolitionism – movement to end slavery
  - 1808 – Congress outlawed the slave trade (illegal to import new slaves)

- o 1817 – American Colonization Society
  - Shipped <u>freed</u> slaves back to Africa (founded present day country, Liberia)
  - Favored by some abolitionists because they felt guilty and ironically by slave owners because they didn't want freed slaves to inspire current slaves
  - Did not work well and fizzles by 1830 or so
- o 1833 – Anti-slavery society formed
- o William Lloyd Garrison – radical/passionate white abolitionist
  - Editor of <u>Liberator</u> newspaper calling for the immediate and uncompensated end of slavery in America
  - Burned a copy of the Constitution saying it was a deal with the devil since it didn't condemn slavery
- o Frederick Douglass – escaped slave who became one of the greatest and most outspoken abolitionists. Wrote his own influential autobiography.
- o Harriet Tubman and Underground Railroad – although only hundreds (out of millions) were freed via the RR, it was the idea that so angered the South, rather than the miniscule number. Hence it helped lead to the Fugitive Slave Act of 1850 which helped lead to the war…
- o See Uncle Tom's Cabin (1852)
- o Grimke sisters – pair of Quakers abolitionist sisters (and women's rights activists)

<u>D. Slavery in United States</u>
- 1793 – invention of cotton gin by Eli Whitney
  - o Slavery was becoming less profitable and may have died out, but with the invention of the cotton gin, suddenly huge profits could be made; thus cotton becomes the number one crop in the south and sustains slavery economically
  - o Huge demand for cotton from New England and English textile mills
  - o Known as "King Cotton" – so profitable it prevents the South from industrializing
- Only ¼ of white families owned slaves in 1860 (2/3 of those owned less than 10 slaves)
  - o Therefore, although most whites didn't own slaves, they supported it because it created status in society
- Justified by…
  - o Arguing slaves are like children needing parents to watch them (paternal view)
  - o Biblical references to slavery
- Slaves were valuable investments – rarely would they be used for the most dangerous work nor purposely killed.
- Rebellions
  - o 1739 – Stono rebellion in S. Carolina (near the Stono River); dozens of slaves attempt to escape to Spanish Florida but are defeated. S.C. passes harsh laws designed to restrict slaves
  - o 1822 – Denmark Vesey in S. Carolina caught planning a rebellion; he and over 30 others are hung in response
  - o 1831 – Nat Turner in Virginia – he and followers killed ~ 60 whites
    - Result was a backlash of even harsher slave laws; forbidden to read/write
    - 1831 is major turning pt. in slavery (same year Liberator 1st published)

6. Expansion and leadup to Civil War

Terms:

- Manifest destiny – it is God's design or purpose for the United States to spread over the continent; to grow from "sea to shining sea"; natives and Mexicans seen as inferior
- Popular sovereignty – territories can decide by vote whether they want slavery or not
    - Proposed by Lewis Cass
    - An attempt to compromise over slavery (just let the people decide! How can they be wrong?!)
- Sectionalism – increased polarization between regions economically, socially, politically and on issues like slavery, foreign affairs, etc. (North/South)

See expansion chart in Topics section for more details

John Tyler (1841-1844) (ex-Democrat but expelled from the Whig party – scandalous!)

Texas Independence

- 1821 – Mexico won independence from Spain
- American settlers encouraged to enter Texas region of Mexico
- By 1835, they far outnumbered Mexicans and conflicts began
- Texas Revolution occurs, 1835 – 36. Battle of the Alamo, San Jacinto, etc.
- Independent Texas Republic 1836 – 1845 (9 years) – led by Sam Houston
    - England was interested in TX as a source of cotton
- Texas annexed in 1845 by the U.S. by John Tyler (opposed by abolitionists)

James K. Polk (1844-1848) (Democrat) – "Young Hickory"

- Oregon
    - Had been jointly occupied by the U.S. and British since the 1818 treaty but now Americans were clamoring for "All or Nothing," and "54° 40″ or Fight!!!" (meaning they wanted Oregon up to the 54th latitude line, well into present day Canada)
    - The U.S. didn't really want to go to war with Great Britain, and vice versa so they compromised on the 49th parallel which is the current border for much of the U.S./Canada line (they share the longest unfortified border in the world!)
- Mexican – American War (1846 – 1848) – known as "Polk's War"
    - President Polk offers to buy California from Mexico for $25 million; Mexico refuses
    - Polk moves American soldiers into the disputed border territory along Texas and MX until they provoke an attack by Mexican soldiers. War is thus declared and the U.S. defeats Mexico, entering Mexico City in 1848.
    - Wilmot Proviso suggested early on: a proposal to ban slavery from any land conq'd from Mexico. It fails to pass because Southerners of course want to spread slavery! (technically, it passes in the House but fails in the Senate)
    - Quick aside: recommendation for a good laugh: search online for "Gadsden Purchase Jimmy Fallon" and find the late night clip featuring the Gadsden Purchase and the Treaty of Guadalupe Hidalgo and you'll get the resulting references I and my students make...and have a great historical laugh!

- o Treaty of Guadalupe – Hidalgo (1848) [who wants to party?!] – U.S. paid Mexico $15 million (to make it seem more legit) and received the <u>Mexican Cession</u> (CA, New Mexico Territory); pretty much all the Southwest
  - ▪ Note: Texas is <u>not</u> part of this acquisition; although its borders were in dispute with Mexico before the war, it had already been annexed in 1845
- o Result of the war was to push the issue of expansion of slavery even more to the forefront; thus it was a major precursor to the Civil War (increasing sectionalism)

Zachary Taylor (1848 – 1850; dies in office) (Whig)
- He was a war hero from the Mexican – American War.
- Remember, most in the North were not strongly opposed to slavery but gradually, especially in the 1850s more people are convinced. Some are simply against its expansion because slaves are competition for free whites in new territories (Free Soil Party)
- CA Gold Rush (1848) – gold is discover at Sutter's Mill
  - o Young men flock there (49ers); lawless
  - o Dramatic population increase and need for a stable government brings up the issue of a quick application for CA statehood (see below). Some were afraid of CA going its own way, so they wanted to fast track this process.

Millard Fillmore (1850 – 52) (Whig)
- Only real importance is that Fillmore was much more ready to sign the Compromise of 1850 than Taylor was
- Compromise of 1850 (5 provisions)
  - o Put together by the "Immortal Trio" – Daniel Webster (North), John C. Calhoun (South), Henry Clay (West). With their subsequent deaths the era of compromise dies too
  - o It's an attempt to balance pro- and anti-slavery views
  1. CA is admitted as a free state
  2. The slave <u>trade</u> is abolished in Washington D.C. (no buying/selling allowed in D.C.)
  3. A stricter Fugitive Slave Act is passed
  4. TX gives up land claims to New Mexico territory and receives $10 million in compensation
  5. Utah and New Mexico territories are created out of the rest of the Mexican Cession and allowed to choose slavery or not via popular sovereignty
  - o The Fugitive Slave Act in particular, the one thing that really benefited the South, was the one item in this Compromise that ultimately angered the North the most and helped lead to the Civil War. Many northerners who did not care much about slavery one way or another, but were now suddenly expected to participate in the capture of runaway slaves, and could be fined or jailed if they helped slaves, became transformed into abolitionists as a result.
  - o Because the Compromise postponed the war for 10 years, it actually worked in the North's favor as in those 10 years more people became motivated against slavery and the North built up its advantages (people and factories); in other words, if secession had happened in 1850, the North might have let the South go…

Franklin Pierce (1852 – 1856) (Democrat)
- Uncle Tom's Cabin (1852) – by Harriet Beecher Stowe
  - o Showed the horrors of slavery; helped convince many in the North

- Lincoln: "so you're the little woman who wrote the book that made this great war"
- Gadsden Purchase (1853) – the U.S. buys a small area of desert land in the Southwest for $10 million. The reason was to allow for a Southern Transcontinental railroad, since the area through the Gadsden Purchase was less mountainous then other parts of Arizona. However, Southerners failed to get the first transcontinental railroad anyway…
  - Because "making fun of the Gadsden Purchase is what life is all about!"
- Kansas – Nebraska Act (1854)
  - KS and NB can choose slavery based on popular sovereignty
  - KS and NB were above the old 36° 30″ line set by the Missouri Compromise so it invalidated it. It was a desperate attempt to create a new balance but failed.
  - Stephen Douglas was a major proponent
- Bleeding Kansas (1855 – 1857)
  - With popular sovereignty now deciding the slavery issue in KS, both pro- and anti-slavery forces flood to KS from around the country in hopes of throwing the vote to their side's favor
  - John Brown massacres some pro-slavery settlers
  - Lecompton Constitution – an illegal pro-slavery constitution they tried to pass

James Buchanan (1856-1860) (Democrat)
- Brooks-Sumner conflict (1856) – anger over slavery spills over onto the Senate floor
  - Southerner Preston Brooks beat northerner Charles Sumner over the head with a cane, making him a hero in the South (that cane-do spirit!)
- The South wanted to spread slavery and turned to Central America
  - 1854 – Ostend Manifesto – a secret Southern plan to offer $120 million to Spain for the purchase of Cuba (to expand slavery there) or to take it by force if Spain refused; the North found out about it and it caused considerable consternation!
  - 1856 – William Walker takes over Nicaragua and declares it open to slavery
    - A group of Latin American countries overthrow him and he is shot
- *Impending Crisis of the South* (1857) – a book by a white southerner that argued against slavery, saying that it really hurt poor non-slave holding whites most of all
- Panic of 1857
  - A downturn in the economy; it hurt the North more than it hurt the South (because cotton sales were still good; Cotton was king!)
  - Gave the South a false sense of strength/confidence before the impending war
- *Dred Scott* decision (1857)
  - Scott sued for his freedom because his master took him into free territory
  - The Supreme Court ruled that since Scott was a slave, he was not a citizen, and therefore could not sue. Furthermore, since all slaves are property, they can be then taken anywhere in the States. This essentially meant that there was no "free" territories and made void all previous agreements the gov't had made to try to regulate expansion of slavery (well I guess that settles that eh? No more problems right? Oy vey!)
- Lincoln – Douglas debates (1858) – a battle for the Illinois Senate seat
  - Issue of slavery a major topic
  - Freeport Doctrine – Douglas argued that popular sovereignty should decide the expansion of slavery not *Dred Scott* decision. So, which has priority: the Supreme Ct. or the will of the people?
  - Lincoln loses the election

- 1859 – <u>John Brown leads a raid on a federal arsenal at Harper's Ferry</u> in Virginia. He was hoping to get weapons and arm slaves for a large-scale revolt. He was captured and hung becoming a hero/martyr for many in the North and a madman to those in the South.
- 1860 – Election of Abraham Lincoln – 3 other parties formed and split the vote thus enabling Lincoln to win even though he didn't win a single Southern state. This was more evidence that the South had no influence in the U.S. government and was thus the final straw to signal secession. South Carolina was the first state to secede.
- Crittenden Compromise – last ditch effort to prevent a split in the union
  - It suggested a line of free north and slave south (like the Missouri Compromise) but it opened slavery all the way to the tip of S. America essentially declaring open season on all countries south of the U.S. (unrealistic and it failed)

7. The Civil War
Abraham Lincoln (1860 – 1865) (Republican)

North	South
Union – blue	Confederacy – grey
Lincoln	Jefferson Davis (President)
Ulysses S. Grant	Robert E. Lee, "Stonewall" Jackson
More factories, population, railroads	Only have to win a defensive war

- April 1861 – Attack on Ft. Sumter – Lincoln wisely sends supplies but not troops to Ft. Sumter, a federal fort in S. Carolina (the Confederacy!), a non-aggressive act, but the Confederates don't want it to remain under Union control so they bombard it and take it over. Thus, the Confederacy "started" the war enabling Lincoln to take the higher ground
- Lincoln's #1 war aim at the outset of the war: preserve the Union, not end slavery
- Union Plan: Anaconda Plan
  - blockade the South, and split it especially by taking the MS river
- Border States – Missouri, Kentucky, Maryland, Delaware… Keeping the border states in the Union is of great importance because their shift to the South would provide the Confederates with more people and factories, and thus perhaps an edge to win the war. Lincoln declares martial law and suspends *habeas corpus* in order to keep them under control. This was especially used against "copperheads," or Southern sympathizers living in the Union.
- Battle of Bull Run (Manassas) (1861)
  - 1st major battle; both sides thought they could win quickly
  - Victory for the South; fed the South's overconfidence; wake-up call to the North
- Trent Affair – (1861) a British ship that was carrying Confederate diplomats; the Union seized the Confederates off the ship. Almost pushed Britain into war with the Union.
- Monitor vs. Merrimack – (1862) two ironclad ships duke it out to a draw. Militarily not that important but important as it begins the process of making wood ships obsolete.
- Battle of Antietam – September 1862 – militarily a draw, but enough of a "victory" for the North to keep Britain and France from diplomatically recognizing the Confederacy and giving them aid (i.e., this battle keeps foreign help out), and enough for Lincoln to issue a preliminary Emancipation Proclamation.
- Emancipation Proclamation – Jan 1. 1863 – It freed slaves only in the rebelling states (i.e., in the Confederate states, not in the slave-holding border states). So, in reality, Lincoln freed slaves where he had no power to do so, and didn't free them where he had

the power to do so. However, more importantly, this now made the war much more about slavery, giving the Union the moral standpoint to pursue victory, and further kept European powers out, since the British and French had both outlawed slavery in their own countries.

- The draft was used during the Civil War; huge riot in New York city in 1863; mostly Irish…
- Battle of Gettysburg (July 1863) – invasion of the North by the South. Ends in Northern victory (disaster of Pickett's Charge); last offensive of the South. It's the major turning point of the war.
- Battle of Vicksburg (July 1863) – one day after the Gettysburg victory, the siege of Vicksburg ends with the South surrendering. Vicksburg is a key city on the Mississippi river thus giving the Union control over that river and more power in the West
- 1864 – Sherman marches to the sea in Georgia – using "total war," he marches across Georgia to the coast at Savannah, further cutting the Confederacy up and demoralizing the enemy
- Election of 1864 – growing successes, especially Sherman in Georgia, as well as strong-arm tactics in the border states helped Lincoln win; gave him a mandate to finish the war
- Appomattox Courthouse (1865) – Lee surrenders to Grant, effectively ending the war
- April, 1865 – Lincoln assassinated by John Wilkes Booth
- Mathew Brady – photographer whose works bring home the horrors of the conflict

8. Reconstruction (1865 – 1877)
- Rebuilding the South physically and socially (or at least that was the intention)

Andrew Johnson (1865-1868) (Republican – sort of…)
- Presidential Reconstruction: Johnson followed Lincoln's intention of being lenient toward the South. His 10% plan only req'd 10% of Confederates pledge their allegiance to the Union. However, Johnson was mostly wanting to lord it over the wealthy planting class that had once looked down upon him, a poor white Southerner growing up. Unlike what we expect Lincoln may have done, Johnson did not support radical improvements for former slaves.
- Congressional Reconstruction – led by the Radical Republicans, they wanted to treat the South harshly. The Wade-Davis Bill they passed required 50% oath allegiance instead of 10%
  o They wanted to reconstruct the South to make it better for African Americans
- Freedmen's Bureau
  o Federal government organization designed to help freedmen with food, clothing, medical care, and education
  o Succeeded mostly in the area of education and literacy; insufficient in other areas
- Black codes
  o Laws that Southern states passed to restrict freedmen / maintain control over them
- Many freedmen were reduced to sharecropping – working someone else's land and being req'd to pay with the crop you produce. Often resulted in eventual debt which became a form of economic slavery. Freedmen became contractually tied to the land.
- Rise of the Ku Klux Klan (KKK)
  o Created to scare freedmen and use violence/fear to control the black population
  o The federal government actually cracked down on the Klan and it became quite small by the end of Reconstruction and only came back into prominence later…

- Amendments passed
  - 13th (1865) – abolishes slavery
  - 14th (1868) – blacks given citizenship; all citizens guaranteed due process of law and equal protection of the law; federal gov't would protect rights if states failed to do so
  - 15th (1870) – cannot be deprived the right to vote based on race or being a former slave (ways to get around this though such as literacy tests, poll taxes, grandfather clause, etc.)
- Reconstruction Act of 1867 (Military Reconstruction)
  - Enacted because many Southern states were not conforming with the Radical Republicans wishes in improving lives of freedmen
  - Created 5 military districts in the South with troops to ensure states complied
  - States had to ratify the 14th amendment and guarantee black suffrage to get the troops to be removed
  - Because many blacks were enabled to vote and many whites boycotted the polls, the result was the election of blacks to various levels of state gov't and Congress
    - Things seem to be quite improving, but…see Compromise of 1877 below
- Impeachment of Johnson (1867 – 1868)
  - Johnson ticked off the Radical Republicans because he was too lenient and didn't care about black reforms
  - They impeached him, which means to put the President on trial. However, he survived by just one vote, and was not removed from office.
  - In the end, it was good that he was not removed, as that would have a set a bad precedent of Congress attempting to remove a President any time they don't like his policies, instead of for "high crimes and misdemeanors" which is the Constitutional bar…
- Carpetbaggers – Southern derogatory term for whites who came from the North to help "rebuild" the South and/or help freedmen; they were often seen as schemers out to make money by running scams on the South or to get federal aid money
- Scalawags (aargh, matey!) – Southern derogatory term for whites who were from the South but worked with the Northerners to "rebuild" the South. They were seen as traitors.
- The "New South" – an attempt to build up the manufacturing ability of the South; generally failed and the South remained agricultural and behind the North for decades

Ulysses Grant (1868 – 1876) (Republican)
- Although a good Civil War general, he was a very ineffective President; known for the many scandals in his administration and his inability to deal with them. Corruption was widespread.
  - Credit Mobilier Scandal – many Congressmen received bribes, causing them to overlook rampant fraudulent practices in building the Transcontinental RR
  - Whiskey Ring scandal – Grant's personal secretary committed fraud

Settlement of the West:
- Homestead Act (1862) passed: gave 160 acres of gov't land to anyone over 21 yrs old, who would build on the land and live there for at least 5 years (purpose: to settle the West)
- Cash subsidies and land grants were given to RR companies to encourage them to build (the total land given was greater than the size of TX)
- Transcontinental Railroad finished in 1869 linking the country.

- Morrill Land Grant of 1862 – gave land grants to states for the formation of public higher education (another foundation of America's good university system)
- Panic of 1873 – a main issue is the printing of money. Farmers wanted more money in circulation to help with debts (This will culminate in the Populist Party [see below]).

Rutherford B. Hayes (1876 – 1880) (Republican)
- Compromise of 1877 (sometimes called the 2nd Corrupt Bargain; Rutherford becomes "Rutherfraud") – Election of 1876 is a close election and there are disputed votes in some southern states. Northern Republicans are desperate to keep the political power of the Presidency, and many northerners, after the Panic of 1873, are more concerned about economic affairs in the North and are getting tired of enforcing reconstruction in the South. Thus, a compromise over the election is reached: the Republicans under Hayes can get the disputed votes, thus winning the election, but they have to pull the remaining troops out of the South and end Reconstruction. With no troops or enforcement of equality by the North, "redeemers" come into power in the Southern state governments and a return to white supremacy and black oppression ensues. Because of this compromise, African Americans effectively lost the hard won gains from the Civil War for 80-90 years until the modern Civil Rights era of the 1950/60s.
- Some have argued that, in the long run, the South could be said to have won the Civil War since they were able to create the society on their terms, i.e. segregation.

9. The Gilded Age (1870ish – 1900)
- A time period of outward prosperity but inward corruption/difficulty for the nation
  - Like "gold-covered poop" – don't actually use that analogy in an essay!!
- **Laissez – faire** – "hands off" – describes the attitude of the gov't not being very involved in the economy. The only time the gov't usually got involved was to help big business and suppress the masses (gov't sends in the troops!)

Captains of Industry (or Robber Barons?!) – the real people in power during the Gilded Age
- Andrew Carnegie – steel; Gospel of Wealth
- J.D. Rockefeller – oil (Standard Oil Company)
- J.P. Morgan – banking
- Cornelius Vanderbilt and Jay Gould (railroads)
- By using horizontal/vertical integration, such men created monopolies and trusts, also manipulating rebates, kickbacks, and other tactics to control their businesses and mercilessly destroy their competition
- Many practiced philanthropy – giving away vast fortunes to help those who could help themselves (Gospel of Wealth – Andrew Carnegie)
- Political machines become very important
  - An organized network that works to get a party or person elected
  - Often involves spoils system; often very corrupt; often used to manipulate and steal money from local governments
  - Usually headed by a "boss" – the most famous was Boss Tweed, head of the political machine at Tammany Hall in New York City
    - Thomas Nast (famous cartoonist) helps bring him down
  - Often takes advantage of immigrant groups – you get my guy elected and I'll make sure your group gets benefits. E.g. all the Irish vote for someone; if he wins, the candidate will make sure the new park or fire station is built in the Irish part of

town. Meanwhile, the Boss and his cronies will then use the influence of that "stooge" politician for their own financial gain.

Major Miscellaneous Gilded Age Topics – Immigration, Strikes, Unions, Native Americans, African Americans

A. Era of "New Immigrants" from southern/eastern Europe including: Italians, Poles, Greeks, Jews from Russia, etc.

- o They were considerably different than "old" immigrants so they faced even more discrimination
- o Many were willing to work for low wages; employed as "scabs" or strikebreakers. They helped build up America's industrial power.
- o Some were "birds of passage," or those who intended to return to their country
- o Many immigrants lived in big cities, in slums and ethnic neighborhoods [ghettos] like Chinatown, Little Italy, etc.
- Nativists opposing immigrants during this era might join the APA, or American Protective Association, which wanted restrictions on immigrants
- To help immigrants with the transition, settlement houses were formed, where immigrants could get job training, English classes, child care, etc. The most famous was the Hull House in Chicago, founded by Jane Addams.
- Urbanization in the Gilded Age saw the massive growth of cities; skyscrapers, trolleys and the beginning of mass transport; many cities became overcrowded, disease ridden. The wealthy tended to move to the suburbs.

B. 4 Major Strikes/Riots of the Gilded Age: (usual theme – gov't sends in the troops!)
- 1877 – National Railroad Strikes – wages were cut 10% so workers went on strike; gov't sent in troops to crush the strike after deaths and destruction
- 1886 – Haymarket Riot – workers were striking in Chicago when someone threw a bomb in the crowd, killing several police. It was blamed on anarchists and associated with the Knights of Labor, leading to their downfall.
- 1892 – Homestead Steel Strike – the Homestead plant was owned by Carnegie; striking workers fought with Pinkerton protected strikebreakers (scabs!); the gov't sent in troops to crush the strike and it failed.
- 1894 – Pullman Strike – workers wages were cut by 1/3 but no corresponding cuts in company housing costs were made. Workers went on strike; overturned and burned railway cars. Ultimately, the federal gov't sent in troops to crush the strike, using the justification that it was to ensure delivery of the mail! Eugene Debs becomes a radical socialist while in jail after this event.

- Work conditions in the Gilded Age continued to be harsh; long hours, low pay, workers had few rights
  - o Yellow-dog contracts (or iron-clad oath) – workers were forced to sign these for employment agreeing they would not join a union
  - o Company towns – workers often lived in towns owned by the company they worked for, paying rent to the company, shopping at the company store; thus the company controlled their lives and money

- Injunctions – issued by the courts, these force workers to go back to work, effectively ending strikes. First used most effectively during the Pullman Strike, business leaders sought these from sympathetic courts.

C. Unions of the Era

Knights of Labor	American Federation of Labor (AFL)
Unskilled + skilled	Skilled only
Leader: Terence Powderly	Leader: Samuel Gompers
More idealistic; wanted workers' utopia	Fought for "bread and butter" issues: higher wages, shorter hours, etc…
Not very successful since unskilled laborers could be replaced easier with scabs; makes it hard to negotiate…	Was more successful since they had only skilled workers

- Closed shops – an agreement or negotiation that unions would demand from employers that said they must hire *only* union members (i.e., jobs are closed to non-union)

D. Jim Crow era
- Jim Crow laws - laws that enforced segregation; lynching common
- 1896 – *Plessy v. Ferguson* – case that established *separate but equal* – legalized segregation!
- Sharecropping kept blacks tied to the land; an economic slavery or servitude

Booker T. Washington (Wait) Vs.	W.E.B. DuBois (Demand)
Born in the South	Born in the North
Economic equality	Political/social equality
Work hard and earn whites' respect	Demand equality
Industrial/vocational training (use hands)	Higher education
Founded Tuskegee Institute	1st black Phd Harvard graduate
	Founded NAACP
	Wanted to develop the "talented tenth"

- "BTW wants to make men into carpenters; I [Dubois] want to turn carpenters into men!"
- Ida B. Wells – African American woman who successfully led a crusade against lynchings

E. Native Americans
- Great Plains Indians were the most notable group during the Gilded Age
- Dependent on the vast herds of buffalo; they used them for food, shelter, clothing…
  - U.S. army recognized that the best way to wipe out the Indian was to wipe out the buffalo. Millions of buffalo eventually dwindled down to just several thousand.
- From 1850 to 1890, tribes were systematically forced onto reservations (usually the poorest, left over land)
- Children were often taken from parents and forced to assimilate
- Dawes Severalty Act (1887)
  - Broke up tribal reservation land into individual family plots (160 acres) – sort of a Homestead Act for Indians
  - It was an attempt to assimilate the natives; make them more like white farmers

- To make things worse, whites would often come later and swindle the individual, unsuspecting Indians out of their already low-quality land
- Helen Hunt Jackson wrote a book called "A Century of Dishonor" in 1881, which discussed the long history of injustices of the U.S. gov't toward Native Americans, such as the many broken treaties they had made…
- Key Battles
  - 1864 – Sand Creek Massacre – despite an American flag and a peace medal given them by President Lincoln, Black Kettle and White Antelope and their Cheyenne followers were massacred by Colonel Chivington and the U.S. army in Colorado
  - 1876 – Battle of Little Bighorn
    - After gold was discovered in the Black Hills of the Dakota territory (and within the Sioux reservation), gold seekers flood the area leading to conflict
    - This led to a huge gathering of natives in nearby Montana. There Colonel Custer and his 264 men stumbled into thousands of native warriors and were massacred. A rare and short-lived victory for Native Americans.
  - 1890 – Massacre at Wounded Knee
    - As U.S. soldiers were disarming some Sioux Indians, a shot rang out and the soldiers began shooting into the crowd of Indians, massacring 128 men, women, and children
    - This was the last major Indian conflict…few major events after this
- The 1890 census is seen as the close of the Frontier; no more line between civilization and non; the West is broken up with settlements
- Frederick Jackson Turner's Frontier Thesis
  - He saw the frontier as a great place of American character development; it shaped the American psyche; it also acted as a "valve" for the East, allowing people to move West rather than lead to revolution when social problems got tense

F. Farmers
- Farmers in the Gilded Age faced many problems from natural disasters, insects, harsh eastern businessmen and railroads, banks threatening to foreclose, etc.
- In an attempt to deal with these challenges farmers created:
  - The Grange
    - Originally promoted social activities among farmers (Grangebook! Haha, that's just a joke like Facebook. I don't want to hear somebody actually put on their essay that the farmers had Grangebook…sigh)
    - Eventually they moved to collectively owning railroads and grain elevators (where they could set their own prices rather than being gouged by the prices of the private companies)
    - *Munn v. Illinois* (1876) – this Supreme Ct. case allowed for states to regulate industries that were in the public good – this means that states could control prices for things that farmers need (railroads for example)
    - *Wabash v. Illinois* (1886) – this Supreme Ct. case put the kibosh on *Munn*. It said that because RRs represent interstate commerce, the states can't regulate them, only Congress could
  - Farmers Alliance – the more politically involved and successor to the Grange
    - Ultimately not very successful; one reason was its exclusion of black farmers
    - The precursor to the Populist Party
  - Populist Party (Populism, or the People's Party) – 1890s

- They believed that most of the farmers' problems stemmed from the lack of money in circulation. It made it hard for them to pay their debts. If inflation could occur, and farm prices went up, they could make more money and more easily pay off their debts.
- The key to this, in their mind, was to have money backed by silver instead of gold as it was then; they wanted free and unlimited coinage of silver.
- They are a significant 3rd party in election of 1892 (in 1896 the Democrats take over their ideas and the Populists die out; see below)

James Garfield (1880 – 1881 – assassinated) (Republican)
- Garfield is assassinated by Charles Guiteau, a disgruntled office seeker, 4 months into his Presidency
- His VP Chester Arthur becomes President

Chester Arthur (1881 – 1884) (Republican)
- 1882 – Chinese Exclusion Act is passed – prevented immigration and restricted rights
- 1883 – Pendleton Act passed. This required many government (civil service) workers to take a test to qualify to work. This represented a major reform to reverse the spoils system (you mean I have to actually know something and not just someone?!).

Grover Cleveland (1884 – 1888) (Democrat)
- He lowered tariffs (he was very laissez – faire) which angered big business; this in turn drove big business into the arms of the Republicans
- Interstate Commerce Commission (ICC) (1887) and Sherman Anti-Trust Act (1890)
  - "Very little teeth" or power.
  - The Sherman Act was supposed to break up big business trusts/monopolies, and anything that "restrained trade"; instead it was used to crush strikes (since they slow trade, etc.)
  - Similarly, during this time, the 14th amendment which guarantees "persons" equal protection of the laws was interpreted to include corporations

Benjamin Harrison (1888 – 1892) (Republican)
- He raised tariffs to appease big business…which angered farmers…so they formed the Populist Party

Grover Cleveland (1892 – 1896) (Democrat)
- Only President to serve two non-consecutive terms
- Panic of 1893 – Depression ruins his Presidency
  - Jacob Coxey – leads a march of men on Washington D.C. demanding the gov't create jobs through public works projects (not unlike the Bonus march of the Great Depression)
    - Gets arrested for standing on the grass (be careful where you tread)

1896 election – William McKinley vs. William Jennings Bryan
- W.J. Bryan gave his famous "Cross of gold" speech, and the Democrats took over the Populists' idea of free silver as the solution to the ills of farmers and others

- Unfortunately, they failed to unite workers with the farmers, and the movement died; McKinley won. They were indeed "crucified upon a cross of gold…" (this is also just a metaphor, no one was actually crucified!)

10. Era of Imperialism (U.S. Expansionism)

[Be aware that imperialism stretches from the Gilded Age into the Progressive Era. It is not between them. It is the foreign affairs complement to these domestic events. Therefore, realize that imperialism events include Spanish American War below but also Panama Canal, Gentlemen's Agreement, etc. all of which happen during the domestic "Progressive Era" see below]

William McKinley (1896 – 1901) (Republican)
    He's assassinated in 1901 by Leon Czolgosz [roughly pronounced Chol-gosh], an anarchist, at the Pan-American Exposition in Buffalo

- Reasons for U.S. imperialism:
    o U.S. needed resources <u>and</u> markets to sell surplus goods in
    o White Man's Burden – the responsibility to provide primitive peoples of the world the law, democracy, and medicine of the white west (Social Darwinism viewpoint)
    o Alfred T. Mahan – author of the book, *"The Influence of Sea Power Upon History"* – it emphasized the importance of strong navy/bases and controlling the seas to have an empire
- Hawaii – seen as a great place for naval base
    o 1893 – American sugar planters, led by Sanford Dole, revolted against Queen Liliuokalani
    o President Cleveland refused to annex it during his Presidency
    o Annexed under McKinley in 1898 (became the 50th state in 1959)

Spanish American War
Causes
1. Yellow Journalism – newspapers would often exaggerate or sensationalize stories to sell more papers (William Randolph Hearst and Joseph Pulitzer were two of the largest paper owners who engaged in this). This desire helped lead to the Spanish-American War because they exaggerated events in Cuba to make profits.
2. De Lome letter – an intercepted letter in which a Spanish diplomat is calling President McKinley weak and other insults
3. *USS Maine* – a U.S. ship in Spanish-owned Cuba that blows up. The U.S. blames Spain and the event is a major cause of the ensuing war. It was probably an accident. "Remember the Maine, to hell with Spain!"

- The war lasts 3 months; the U.S. loses few lives (more die from disease than combat)
- Teddy Roosevelt and the Rough Riders go to Cuba; charge up San Juan Hill to glory
- Admiral Dewey uses the U.S. steel fleet to smash the wooden Spanish fleet in the Philippines
- Known as "A splendid little war"
- The war ends with the Treaty of Paris; the U.S. wins but pays Spain $20 Million and acquires Puerto Rico, Guam, control of Cuba, and ultimately the Philippines

- Teller amendment – the U.S. promised Cuba her independence upon U.S. victory, but changed that with the Platt amendment which wrote into the Cuban Constitution that the U.S. can come back and intervene whenever it was thought necessary (You Teller what you're gonna do [give Cuba independence], but then change your mind and Platt her on the head [threaten intervention]
- The Filipinos were grateful for liberation from the Spanish but America did not give them their independence. Therefore, there was a guerilla war for independence.
  - Led by Emilio Aguinaldo; brutal conflict
  - Revolt eventually fizzled out by 1901
- Anti-Imperialist League formed
  - Argued that imperialism violated American principles (such as rights and freedoms in the Declaration of Independence)
- *Insular* cases – do Constitutional rights extend to people in captured colonies?
  - The Supreme Ct. ruled no ("the Constitution does not outrun the flag")
- China – Open Door Policy (1899) – because European countries had already started carving out "spheres of influence" in China, the U.S. felt like it was late to the game. So, they declared an Open Door Policy that every nation should have equal access to China's market of millions of people. The big loser: China.

11. Progressive Era (~1900 to 1920, ending with WWI basically)

- After McKinley is assassinated in 1901, that "damned cowboy," Theodore Roosevelt, becomes President
- The Progressive Era was a response to the Gilded Age. Solutions to the excesses and injustices of the Gilded Age were sought after in the Progressive Era. It's the beginning of the recognition that as society becomes increasingly complex with urban societies, the role of the federal gov't must increase to provide solutions. In other words, where the Gilded Age gov't was laissez-faire and generally uninvolved in people's lives, during the Progressive Era the government is seen as the agent of improving human welfare.

To keep it simple, information during the Progressive Era is divided up between Domestic Affairs and Foreign Affairs (continuing imperialism)

A. Domestic Affairs – Progressive themes included more fairness in business, more accountability in gov't to the people, conservation of resources, and improvements in the daily lives of people; also, the application of scientific principles to the problems of the day.

Theodore "Teddy" Roosevelt (1901 – 1908) (Republican)
- Very activist President
- Square Deal – more of a fair deal between big business and labor; no longer will government always take the side of big business
  - 3 C's
    - Control of corporations
    - Consumer protection (see *The Jungle* results below)
    - Conservation of natural resources
  - Anthracite coal strike (1902)
    - Mine owners and workers could not reach agreement on the strike
    - Coal was needed for heating during the winter; therefore, it's in the public interest to resolve this crisis

- TR threatened to use the army to work the mines (with the owners not profiting); first time the power of the gov't sided with the workers instead of owners
- Owners gave in and gave workers some concessions (10% pay; 9-hours)
  - Regulated railroads
    - Elkins Act (1903) – forbade railroads from granting rebates to big shippers
    - Hepburn Act (1906) – authorized the ICC to fix maximum rates
  - Trustbuster!
    - Believed in good trusts and bad trusts (obviously only bust the bad ones)
    - Broke up Northern Securities Railroad monopoly owned by JP Morgan
  - Conservation
    - Newlands Act (1902) – sold public lands and used funds for irrigation and reclamation projects (helped transform the arid West and Southwest)
    - Set aside 125 million acres of forest reserves
    - Gifford Pinchot, his head of forestry, and TR agreed that nature must be conserved but not always preserved;

- Muckrakers – journalists who expose problems in society
  - Upton Sinclair
    - Wrote *The Jungle* (1906) – a book that was supposed to demonstrate the problems of capitalism and urge people to socialism
    - What most people took from it, however, was its information on how disgusting the meatpacking plants were: "He aimed for their hearts but hit them in the stomach"
    - It led to significant laws like the Meat Inspection Act and Pure Food and Drug Act
  - Jacob Riis – wrote "How the Other Half Lives" which showed the terrible living conditions of the poor in the cities
  - Lincoln Steffens – wrote "Shame of the Cities" – articles in McClure's magazine about government corruption in cities
  - Ida Tarbell – wrote "The History of Standard Oil Company" which exposed Rockefeller's practices in his oil company

- Improving government
  - Goal was to reduce corruption and make the gov't more democratic, more accessible to the people
  - Initiative – allowed voters to sign a petition to put a proposal on a ballet for a vote (not having to wait for their representatives to do it)
  - Referendum – the people can directly approve or reject laws
  - Recall – voters can vote to remove an elected official
  - 17th amendment (1913) – direct election of Senators (see amendments section)
  - Secret balloting introduced (known as Australian ballot)
  - Direct primaries – an election within a party to pick that party's favorite candidate
  - Robert La Follette – governor of Wisconsin; he was responsible for Progressive state reforms

William Howard Taft (1908 – 1912) (Republican)
- TR's handpicked successor

- Ticked off TR by firing Gifford Pinchot, raising tariffs, trying to bust U.S. Steel (a good trust according to TR) and generally not being as progressive as TR envisioned him to be
- Taft actually busted more trusts than TR and was at least as good a conservationist
- Triangle Shirtwaist Factory Fire (1911)
  - Low paid female immigrants working in textile factory on upper building floors
  - Managers had locked some of the doors going out to prevent unscheduled breaks and to keep union organizers out
  - A fire broke out and within ½ hour over 100 women died from fire, smoke, and from jumping/falling out of the building.
  - It led to improved safety standards, union growth…tragedy led to reforms! Progress!!

- Election of 1912 – TR returns to run for a 3rd term
  - Taft (Republican)
  - T. Roosevelt (Progressive) (also known as the "Bull Moose Party")
    - New Nationalism – increased gov't regulation of business
  - Woodrow Wilson (Democrat)
    - New Freedom – reduction of gov't; fragmentation of big business; give people and small businesses more freedom (less gov't control)
  - TR and Taft split the Republican vote and Wilson wins
  - Significant election as it was a battle of governing philosophies; which type of Progressivism will prevail?

Woodrow Wilson (1912 – 1920) (Democrat)
- Underwood Tariff (1913) – reduced tariffs
- 16th amendment (1913) – with less money from reduced tariffs, the 16th amendment created a federal income tax to raise revenue
- Federal Reserve Act (1913) – created 12 regional banks that help keep the economy stable (current system today)
- Clayton Anti-trust Act (1914) – similar to the old Sherman Act, but with some teeth!

B. Foreign Affairs during the Progressive Era (a continuation of imperialism)
Theodore Roosevelt
- Big Stick Policy – TR said "speak softly and carry a big stick" which meant have a strong military, especially navy, and you can intimidate the world
- Roosevelt Corollary – an addition to the Monroe Doctrine that stated the U.S. could intervene in Latin American countries to keep them stable and make sure they paid their debts (as opposed to European countries coming and doing it, as that would violate the Monroe Doctrine)
- Panama Canal (started in 1904, completed in 1914 after TR)
  - During the Spanish-American War, the USS Oregon had to sail around S. America to get to the combat; took weeks
  - A canal would improve military and maritime trade capability
  - Panama was a part of Columbia which did not want to allow the U.S. to build a canal…simple solution: how's about a revolution Panama?!? The U.S. supported a Panamanian revolution. Once the revolution was done, Panama gave the U.S. permission to build and authority over the canal.

- Russo-Japanese conflict (1905) – TR helped negotiate peace between Russia and Japan (Treaty of Portsmouth) getting the Nobel Peace Prize as a result
- Gentleman's Agreement (1907)
  - San Francisco schools were segregating Japanese school children, angering the Japanese (Americans were afraid of Asian immigration; "yellow peril"). Japan was the most industrialized Asian nation so they didn't like this treatment.
  - TR negotiated with Japan to reduce its immigration to the U.S. in return for San Francisco repealing its segregation practice
- Voyage of the Great White Fleet (1907) – several battleships sent around the world to demonstrate American power

Taft
- "Dollar Diplomacy" – idea was to use trade and American investments to influence Latin American countries toward favorable American policies. Less force and more money: using dollars instead of the military.

Wilson
- "Moral Diplomacy" – intervention in Latin America should be for the "right" and "just" reasons
- 1910 – 1920 – Mexico was going through a revolution; the U.S. sometimes intervened, not supporting Huerta, but supporting Carranza against him. Pancho Villa, a competitor to Carranza, resented this and launched a raid across the American border killing several Americans.
  - Wilson sent John "Blackjack" Pershing after Villa but he had to pull out eventually because of the onset of WWI
- Unsurprisingly, Latin American countries resented much of the U.S. interference during this era

12. World War I (1914 – 1918)
- During Woodrow Wilson's Presidency
- Prior to U.S. entry, Wilson ran in the 1916 election on the campaign slogan, "He kept us out of war"
- Reasons for U.S. entry
  1. Allied trade (Britain/France) was more valuable; that is, the U.S. traded far more with them than Germany; part of that reason is because Britain was blockading Germany and seizing American ships. This angered America, but even more so was…
  2. Germany's unrestricted submarine warfare: Germans submarines (U-boats) sank any ship without warning. At one point, they stopped this with the *Sussex Pledge*, promising to warn ships but eventually went back on this pledge. The most famous ship they sank was the Lusitania, in which 128 Americans died.
  3. Zimmerman Note – Germany proposed an alliance with Mexico to attack the U.S. in return for land from the Mexican Cession. Mexico was busy with its own revolution so the idea never went anywhere, but it was discovered and further alarmed/angered Americans.

- U.S. enters in April 1917 on the side of the Allies (Britain, France, Russia) vs. the Central Powers (Germany, Austria-Hungary, Ottoman Empire)

- Wilson wanted the war to be "the war to end all wars" and to "make the world safe for democracy"
  - To this end, he proposed 14 Points, or a master plan to prevent future wars from happening. They included: freedom of trade and of the seas, self-determination for colonies, an end to secret treaties, and most importantly, the League of Nations.
- John "Blackjack" Pershing led the American Expeditionary Force (AEF) into WWI in France. The other Allies wanted to split American forces up and spread them along the front, but America insisted on keeping U.S. forces together.
- Russian Revolution (1917) – Russia turns to communism under Vladimir Lenin and his Bolshevik party, creating the Union of Soviet Socialist Republics (USSR) or Soviet Union. They subsequently drop out of the war.
- At Home
  - The U.S formed a Committee on Public Information led by George Creel
    - It issued propaganda to support the war; buy liberty bonds, dislike German music/food; 4-minutemen gave patriotic speeches; instituted a draft
  - Cracked down on dissenters: Espionage (illegal to do many things against the war effort; e.g. interfere with recruitment) and Sedition Acts (illegal to use "disloyal, profane…language" against the gov't)
  - Food Administration Board: encouraged voluntary help – Meatless Tuesdays, liberty gardens; other government boards formed to save fuel, etc.
  - *Schenck v. U.S.* – 1919, after the war; the Espionage/Sedition Acts seemed to violate 1st amendment but the Supreme Ct. confirmed the right of the gov't to restrict speech if it created a "clear and present danger"; just like yelling "fire" in a theater does
- End of the War
  - Treaty of Versailles – ends WWI; it blames Germany and forces them to pay reparations; restricts Germany's military; this later gives fuel for Hitler
  - Republicans ("irreconcilables") get control of Congress and reject the Treaty of Versailles and refuse to join the League of Nations (dooming it to failure)

13. The 1920s (1920 – 1929 [go figure!])

A. The Conservative Backlash

- Red Scare – there was a fear of communist influence in America after the Communist Revolution in Russia (1917). Anything resembling pro-labor was considered too liberal and pro-communist (workers unite!). Thus it applied to the things below: immigrants, etc.
- *Buford* (1919) (a.k.a. the "Soviet Ark) – a ship that was sent to the USSR full of deported anarchist and pro-communist supporters
- Emergency Quota Act of 1921 – made a quota that limited the number of immigrants to 3% of how ever many were in the U.S. as of the 1910 census.
- 1924 National Origins Act – revised the quota to 2% of the 1890 census. Result: Reduced some (undesirable "New Immigrants") while keeping others (British)
- Rise of the KKK – this was the heyday of the Klan, i.e., its largest size ever with millions of members. It was supported by WASPs (White, Anglo-Saxon, Protestants) and was against anyone not like them! It declined by the late 1920s.
- A. Mitchell Palmer – Attorney General – he hunted down suspected communists
- Sacco and Vanzetti – a couple of radical Italian anarchists who were arrested for murder and electrocuted (shocking, eh?!). However, it was based on weak evidence, so most

people believe they were really convicted to make an example of rejection of radical views and being immigrants (the Red Scare!).

- Scopes "Monkey" Trial
  - In Dayton, TN, John T. Scopes willingly taught evolution in violation of state law
  - Clarence Darrow defended him
  - William Jennings Bryan (yes, that W.J.B.) argued for the prosecution
  - It was a national media sensation; fundamentalism vs. modernism; the old and new collide!

- Prohibition (18th amendment) (1919) – enforcement was detailed by the Volstead Act (this outlined the actual details how the 18th amendment would work)
  - People rebelled by making their own alcohol (bootleggers) or going to "speakeasies," or illegal bars
  - Gave rise to organized crime/gangs and people like Al Capone (arrested for tax evasion)
  - In the end, proved so difficult to enforce, this "noble experiment" failed
  - Repealed with the 21st amendment in 1933
  - See additional info in the Miscellaneous sections

B. Economics
- "Roaring 20s" – the economy was booming
  - Benefited from the rise of the automobile – changed society; created many jobs
    - Henry Ford revolutionized their production using assembly line methods
    - Result was cars became much more affordable
  - The economy was based on a lot of consumer spending; and this was dependent on "buying on credit"; buy now, pay later!
  - This in turn fueled overproduction; factories were churning out lots of stuff; but buying much of it on credit was only creating a false bubble of prosperity…

C. Miscellaneous 20s stuff
- 19th amendment (1920) – granted women's suffrage
- Charles Lindbergh – famous aviator – he was the first to fly non-stop, solo over the Atlantic. Seen as a hero. His plane was named the Spirit of St. Louis (you can see it today in the Air and Space Museum of the Smithsonian).
- Amelia Earhart – female version of Lindbergh – disappeared while flying over the Pacific
- Flappers – women who challenged traditional expectations – they cut their hair, smoked, drank, wore shorter skirts (Hello! Check out that ankle!!)
- Margaret Sanger –advocated use of birth control – quite radical for the time; argued that women were enslaved to men because of the cycle of pregnancy and childrearing
- Radio – became the must have item of the 20s; contributed to the standardization (or process of becoming similar) across America: many people listening to the same thing
- Marcus Garvey – African American leader who promoted black self-sufficiency (shop at black owned businesses) and the "Back to Africa" movement
  - Created the Universal Negro Improvement Association (UNIA)
  - Had his own Black Star line of shipping to take blacks back to Africa
  - Significant black leader between the eras of DuBois/Washington and MLK/Malcolm X.

- o In the end, he was arrested for fraud and deported.
- Expression
  - o Jazz – with lots of Southern, African-American roots, it became the music of the decade
  - o Harlem Renaissance – outpouring of African American literary expression
    - Langston Hughes – famous poet
  - o Lost Generation – disillusioned after WWI, these writers rejected the materialism and "live it up" consumer mentality of much of America in the 20s
    - F. Scott Fitzgerald, Ernest Hemingway, and others

D. Politics
Warren G. Harding (1920 – 1923; dies in office) (Republican)
- Upon his election he said it was time for America to "return to normalcy," meaning mostly to stop this liberal Progressive nonsense and involvement in world affairs and get back to laissez-faire big business economics and isolationism
- Scandal – ridden administration – not so much him, but the people around him; often compared to Ulysses S. Grant's Presidency
  - o Teapot Dome Scandal – bribery of gov't figure over oil reserves in Wyoming

Calvin Coolidge (1923 – 1928) (Republican)
- "The business of America is business!" – this sums up "Silent Cal"
- One cartoon shows businesses singing, "Oh what a friend we have in Coolidge…" a reference to the gospel lyrics, "Oh what a friend we have in Jesus." I.e., Coolidge continues the pro-business policies that lead to the Roaring 20s (and the Great Depression!)

Herbert Hoover (1928 – 1932) (Republican)

E. Foreign policy during the 20s
- Isolationism! Remember the rejection of the League of Nations?!
- Washington Naval Conference (1921) led to the Five Power Treaty
  - o Established a ratio of tonnage for ships (5:5:3 – U.S., Britain, Japan respectively)
  - o Japan gets a deal that the U.S. and Britain won't fortify bases in the Pacific
- Dawes Plan (1924)
  - o As Germany struggled to pay its debts under the Versailles Treaty, the U.S. rescheduled their payments so Germany owed the U.S. instead of Britain/France

F. End of the 1920s
- October 29, 1929 – "Black Tuesday" – Stock market crashes, wiping out billions of dollars of investment (on paper), sending the economy into a nose dive
- Hawley-Smoot Tariff (1930) – to protect fragile American companies because of the Depression, Congress raised tariffs to one of the highest levels ever. The result was European countries did the same thing, world trade slowed further, and the Depression worsened.

14. The Great Depression and New Deal Era (1929 – 1939ish)

A. Causes, Hoover, and severity of depression

- Causes:
    - Overproduction – factories were making too much that was ultimately bought on credit
    - Buying on credit – when companies/banks called in their loans, people couldn't pay them back
        - Buying on margin – when you buy stock with a small down payment and the rest with credit; great if the stock goes up; not so if it goes down.
    - Uneven distribution of wealth – too much money in the hands of a few

- Hoover preached self-reliance, rugged individualism, private charities, no gov't doles
- He enacted the Reconstruction Finance Corporation (RFC) in which the gov't loaned money to big corporations, banks, etc. and the benefits would "trickle down" to the masses
    - Not much effect on the average person
- Thus Hoover becomes synonymous with failure in the Depression: Hoover blankets (newspaper used as blankets); Hoovervilles (shanty towns for housing)
- Bonus March (1932) – WWI veterans marched on D.C. demanding their bonuses from WWI that weren't due to them until 1945. "We need them now!" – the march was crushed when the veterans (old army) was forced out by the current soldiers
- Hoover loses dramatically to FDR in 1932
- Thousands of banks go out of business
    - Bank runs – people literally run to the bank to get their money out before it runs out
- Approximately 25 – 30% of people unemployed at the height of the Depression
- Men abandoned families; committed suicide (hotel room: "for sleeping or jumping?")
- The Dust Bowl
    - A large area of the Great Plains affected by poor farming practices, drought, and severe wind storms throughout the decade of the 30s
    - Result was huge dust storms across the area
    - "Okies" and "Arkies" and others moved west because things were so desperate

Franklin Delano Roosevelt (1932 – 1945 dies shortly into 4th term) (Democrat)

B. The New Deal

- FDR's plan to get America out of the Great Depression
- 3 R's: Relief, Recovery, and Reform (short, middle, long-term solutions)
- Inaugural Address: "the only thing we have to fear is fear itself!" – reassuring to people
- 1st Hundred Days – Congress passes huge amounts of legislation, following the President's lead (they essentially do whatever he suggests, as everyone is desperate)
- Fireside chats – using the radio, FDR explained to America his plans in various "chats"
- Bank Holiday – closed the banks for several days to calm people and prevent further bank runs. Message: trust the banks once more…
- One of the most important things to understand is how the New Deal expanded the role of the federal gov't. Suddenly the gov't is getting much more involved in the lives of people, and spending a lot more money (deficit spending: spending more than one earns, thus creating debt)! The gov't has grown much larger up to the present since the New

Deal began. Some saw this as an over-extension and worse, a movement towards a gov't run society…socialism!! (Egads, scandalous!!) Thus, this is controversial still today…

- Huey Long of Louisiana (the "Kingfish") was one of the critics of the New Deal, although he was more radical than FDR. He was eventually assassinated.
  - Share the Wealth – a plan to take fortunes from the rich and redistribute a set amount to all Americans (that's radical!)

New Deal Agencies (there were many but I've listed what I think are the most important and shortened it to keep it straight and easy to remember).

- AAA – Agricultural Adjustment Act – since farmers were overproducing, thus lowering prices (supply and demand), the gov't under the AAA paid farmers subsidies to not farm or to farm less. This would help raise prices but was controversial since many people were in need of food and help.
- CCC – Civilian Conservation Corps – a program to put young men from cities to work out in the wilderness building trails, restoring beaches, etc. It kept them from turning to crime and helped sustain them and their families during these troubled years. Critics, however, accused the Corps of paying people to simply push dirt around.
- FDIC – Federal Deposit Insurance Corporation – with this, the <u>federal</u> gov't was <u>insuring</u> (guaranteeing) people's money in the bank (<u>deposits</u>). That way, no need to run down and pull your money out (most big banks today are members of FDIC).
- PWA – Public Works Administration – $3.3 billion for highways, federal buildings, etc.
  - CWA – Civil Works Administration (similar)
- SEC – Security and Exchange Commission – regulates the stock market to hopefully prevent any future stock market crash
- TVA – built dams along the Tennessee valley to produce cheap electricity, prevent erosion, and create jobs for impoverished rural areas in that region
  - Generally lots of benefits but it also represented the gov't competing with private electricity providers; gov't competing with private business? That's socialism!! Oh no!!!!! (not really, but it's more socialistic than just letting private enterprise figure it out…but not many people may get the help they desperately need then…I could go on).

2nd New Deal (after 1935, other measures to help the economy)

- WPA – Works Progress Administration
  - Federal dollars spent to put people to work; notable as it included support of the arts, employing artists, writers, musicians, etc.
- Social Security Act – a safety network to provide for people in need (a radical new idea in America)
  - Provides retirement (money set aside from paychecks paid out after retirement)
  - Support for the unemployed
  - Support for the disabled

- Court Packing Scheme (1937)
  - The Supreme Court struck down several New Deal programs as unconstitutional
  - To overcome this, FDR suggested one justice be added for every one of them over the age of 70 (this would increase the court from 9 to 15)

- o Essentially this was an attempt by FDR to circumvent the separation of powers and checks/balances principles of the Constitution. It never passed, and some saw FDR as acting like a dictator.
- o Eventually the issue was resolved as the court loosened up and stopped blocking as many of his ideas
- Overall legacies of the New Deal are increased gov't involvement, the beginning of the Democratic Party having a greater representation of minorities, urban areas, and the poor, and preventing the Depression from getting worse. New Deal spending didn't end the Depression though (it relieved it); it was WWII spending that ended the Gr. Depression.

C. Leadup to World War II – 1930s foreign policy stuff

- Good Neighbor Policy – under FDR, the U.S. gov't begins to pull troops out of Latin American countries
- Isolationist policies continue in the 1930s
- 1931 – Japan invades Manchuria – the League of Nations does nothing demonstrating its weakness
- 1934 – Nye commission – this panel concludes that it was munitions manufacturers that got the U.S. into WWI by supplying weapons ("merchants of death"); thus the U.S. should not trade with warring countries…which lead to…
- 1935 – 1937 Neutrality Acts – these forbid loans or weapons sales to countries at war, and prevent Americans from sailing on vessels of belligerent (at war) nations (the U.S. doesn't want to get sucked in to a foreign war again)
- 1937 – Panay Incident – Japan attacks an American gunboat (the Panay) in China; Japan apologizes and pays money and America does nothing else about it (Japan appeased?)
- 1935 – 1939 – Hitler begins to break the Versailles Treaty limitations – Germany builds up its military, occupies the Rhineland, Austria, Sudetenland, and Czechoslovakia
  - o Each time Hitler promises not to do it again…each time European powers appease him, that is, give into these actions, hoping that it will be the last…proves foolish!
- Sept. 1, 1939 – Germany invades Poland – WWII begins
  - o Only after signing a non-aggression pact with the USSR; Stalin and Hitler agree to divide up Poland
- Germany captures France and the rest of Europe except Britain
- Germany wages an air war (Battle of Britain) in preparation for an invasion of Britain but fails
- Germany invades the Soviet Union (1941) – Operation Barbarossa
- Many in America want to help Britain since they share a great deal of heritage and they don't want to see the Nazis win
  - o America First Committee – argued America should only worry about American security and not get involved – Charles Lindbergh is a famous member
  - o Gradually, the U.S. moves to helping Britain:
    - Cash and carry policy – the U.S. will sell weapons to Britain and others but they have to pay cash (no loans) and carry it on their own ships
    - Destroyers for bases deal; Britain becomes more desperate: ok, we'll trade you 50 destroyers (small warships) for bases in the Caribbean
    - Finally, Britain can't afford cash-carry, so FDR moves to the Lend-Lease option: the U.S. will provide weapons/supplies for the British to "borrow." The U.S. is going to be the "arsenal of democracy" – basically back to the same problem during WWI…

- The U.S. declares an oil embargo on Japan, hoping that by reducing their access to oil, it will slow Japanese expansion in the Pacific
- Dec. 7th, 1941 – Japan attacks the U.S. at Pearl Harbor; a "date which will live in infamy." Fortunately for the U.S., all 3 vital aircraft carriers are at sea and not damaged.

15. U.S. entry into World War II (1941 – 1945)

A. Home Front

- War Production Board – just as in most major wars, the gov't must get involved and direct the economy
- Japanese Americans were put into internment camps as America felt it was militarily necessary because they might help Japan during an invasion (no evidence)
  - Many were American citizens, but it didn't matter
  - This was upheld in the Supreme Court case, *Korematsu v. U.S.* (1944)
  - In 1988, the U.S. gov't apologized and gave survivors $20,000
  - Many Japanese American young men served in the famous 442nd Infantry Regiment (most decorated regiment unit in the U.S. army) while their families were interned back home
- African Americans
  - Great Migration – African Americans moved to the north in record numbers finding war jobs in major cities (as often is the case, this led to racial tension)
  - A. Philip Randolph – threatened a march on Washington D.C. because of discrimination; FDR created the Fair Employment Practices Commission to help satisfy him
  - Blacks still had to serve in segregated units in the military
  - Tuskegee airmen – famous group of black aviators (pilots)
- Women filled in for men in factories (Rosie the Riveter); served in support military roles (WAVES – navy; WAAC/WAC – army, etc)
- *Braceros* program – the U.S. encouraged Mexican immigration as farm laborers
  - Zoot suit riots – Mexican American youth clashed with military servicemen in Los Angeles
- Native Americans – thousands served in the military, including some Navajo as "codetalkers"

B. The War itself

- Atlantic Charter (1941) – FDR and Churchill met off the coast of Newfoundland to plan a vision for the post-war world (WWII's version of the 14 Points)
- Casablanca Conference (Jan. 1943) – the Big Three (FDR, Churchill, Stalin) meet and agree on demanding unconditional surrender from the Axis
- Tehran Conference (Nov. 1943) – the Big Three discuss opening up a 2nd front in Europe (to take pressure off the Soviets)
- Yalta Conference (Feb. 1945) – Stalin promises free elections in Poland after the war; he does not keep this promise later on. They agree to the formation of a United Nations.
- Potsdam Conference (July 1945) – the Big Three (Truman instead of FDR) meet and demand Japan's unconditional surrender

European Theater

- North Africa is the first place the Allies push back the Nazi juggernaut; leads to the invasion of Italy

- D-Day (June 6th, 1944) – Allied invasion of Normandy, France. The liberation of Europe begins! (Dwight Eisenhower was the Supreme Commander)
- Battle of the Bulge (Dec. 1944) – a last-ditch effort by German forces to push back the Allies; it creates a bulge in the Allied lines, but eventually is forced back
- Germany surrenders on May 7th, 1945 (V-E Day – Victory in Europe)

Pacific Theater
- General Douglas MacArthur and the U.S. army are forced out of the Philippines by the Japanese in 1942
  - "I shall return" he famously said
  - After the Battle of Leyte Gulf (1944), he said, "I have returned Philippines!"
  - Bataan Death March – U.S. and Filipino prisoners are marched many miles; many are killed along the way
- Battle of Midway (June 1942) – turning point in Pacific war; U.S. destroys 4 Jap. Carriers
- Island – hopping strategy – jump over some islands and only fight to seize the most strategically important islands leading the way to an invasion of Japan
- Other battles: Coral Sea, Guadalcanal, Leyte Gulf, Iwo Jima, Okinawa…
- Manhattan Project – name for the development of the atomic bomb
- The U.S. dropped two atomic bombs on Japan:
  - Aug. 6th on the city of Hiroshima
  - Aug. 9th on the city of Nagasaki
  - Truman never questioned their use, arguing that it saved more lives in the end because it ended the war quickly and prevented the need for a long and deadly invasion of Japan (possibly also to intimidate the Soviets, who were a rising potential enemy)
- Japan surrendered on Aug. 14th, 1945 (V-J Day; Victory in Japan)

- The U.S. and Soviet Union gradually emerge as the two "Superpowers"

16. The Cold War through JFK

A. Miscellaneous Post WWII and 50s Culture info (not really Cold War but during the same time!)
- GI Bill (1944) – paid for returning veterans college expenses and provided low-interest loans for houses/businesses (by putting many into college, it helped prevent major unemployment as millions of veterans returned to the U.S. from the war)
- 50s and 60s – great economic prosperity (dramatic increase in standards of living)
  - Based on large gov't military spending (industrial military complex; arms race!)
  - Also on lots of consumer spending (automobiles, televisions, appliances, etc.)
- The Baby Boom – 1945 – 1960 – major increase in the birth rate
  - Many baby-boomers are retiring now and one consequence is the shrinking of Social Security as too many people are drawing from the pool of money
- Taft-Hartley Act (1947)
  - Anti-labor bill; weakened unions and strikes
- Rise of the suburbs – dramatic movement to the suburbs during booming post-war economy
  - Levittowns – "cookie-cutter" housing; cheap and mass-produced
  - White flight – many of those fleeing to the suburbs were white; the result was the degradation of the inner-cities as much of the wealth was removed
- Growth of the sunbelt

- o Large migration to southern, southwestern, southeastern ("sun") states;
- o Availability of air conditioning is one major factor that allows this demographic change
- Women were expected to be married and take care of her home, husband, and children; a new "Cult of domesticity" developed
  - o Rebellion to this gradually developed; the rise of feminism and the sexual revolution of the late 60s
  - o Betty Friedan – wrote a book, "The Feminine Mystique" (1963) – gave voice to women's dissatisfaction with this traditional role. "Is this all?" she asked.
- Television – a major consumer good of the 50s; eventually affects the unpopularity of the Vietnam War and contributes to the success of the Civil Rights movement
- Rock n' Roll – emerging music of the youth; Elvis – the King; the music was seen as corrupting the youth
- Beatniks (50s) – non-conformists; the "hipsters"; meeting in cafes, reading poetry, expressing themselves; not settling for a white collar office job that was popular at the time. Precursor to the counterculture and hippy movement of the 60s. Jack Kerouac was one of the most famous of the beatniks. (parallels to the Lost Generation of the 20s).
- The 50s are often seen by conservatives as a happy, joyous era where things were the way they "were supposed to be"; liberals tend to see it as a repressive, conformist era.

B. Real Cold War stuff
- Nuremberg Trials – trials of Nazi leaders. It is the 1st time war leaders were held accountable for war crimes.
- With WWII over, Germany is split into West and East Germany
- In addition, the Soviet Union refuses to withdraw from Eastern Europe. Instead it forces these nations (E. Germany, Poland, Romania, etc) to follow communism.
- The Cold War: The Cold War starts where WWII left off. Germany and Japan are defeated, but the new threat is the Soviet Union (USSR). This rising nation threatens to spread communism around the world (scandalous!). The Cold War is a faceoff between the U.S. and the Soviet Union. It is referred to as "cold" because the two nations never directly confront one another militarily, that is, get into a "hot" fight or attack each other. There are some wars (Korean, Vietnam) but these are called "proxy wars," meaning the two nations fight *through* other nations, each supporting one side or the other. Instead, the Cold War (lasting approx. 45 years) is a struggle or competition to outdo each other. The two nations compete in an arms (weapons) race, nuclear race, space race, and more. It dominates foreign affairs for most of 1945 – 1991.

Harry S Truman (1945 – 1952) (Democrat)
- Truman's "Fair Deal" – expands some social security benefits but otherwise is not very effective
- 2nd Red Scare – just like after WWI there was a Red Scare, there is a Red Scare after WWII. A fear of communists amongst us. This manifests itself in several ways:
  - o HUAC (House of Un – American Activities Committee) – (most notably active in the late 1940s and 50s) – A House of Representatives group that investigated the loyalty of Americans. Most memorable were the accusations of those in Hollywood being communists. Many were blacklisted (put on a list of suspects) and unable to work.

- - Alger Hiss case (1948 – 1950) – Alger Hiss was a well known gov't official who was accused of being a communist. A young Richard Nixon helped imprison him on perjury charges (lying under oath). It seemed to confirm to people the potential for communists among us. Hiss's guilt and case are still controversial to this day…
    - Joseph McCarthy (1950 – 53) – a U.S. Senator who had hearings and investigations that accused people of being communists. He claimed to have a list of 205 known communists working in the U.S. gov't. When he started accusing military officials, the "witch hunt" finally fizzled.
    - Julius/Ethel Rosenberg (1951 – 53) – convicted of stealing atomic secrets and giving them to the Soviets, they were electrocuted (ooh, similar to Sacco/Vanzetti?!) (shocking again, I know!).
- "Iron Curtain" – the phrase used by Churchill to describe how the Soviets have spread communism and their harsh rule over much of Eastern Europe
- Truman Doctrine – as communism begins to spread and fear in America increases (special concerns in Greece/Turkey), Truman declares that the U.S. will help any country that will resist communism (with money, military support, etc.). The main goal is to contain communism.
- Marshall Plan (1947) – there was a lot of concern that communism would spread to Western Europe, so to help "contain" it, the U.S. pledged billions of dollars of aid to France, Britain, etc. to help rebuild after the war, if they promised not to follow communism.
- Berlin Airlift (1948-49) – Stalin cut off supplies to West Berlin, so the U.S. airlifted supplies to the city for 1 year to keep it going (the first Cold War showdown)
- 1949 – The Soviets develop the atomic bomb and China falls to communism…a major year of failure of containment. Oops!
- NATO (1949) – North Atlantic Treaty Organization – a group of nations along the Atlantic Ocean (The U.S., Canada, Western Europe) that band together for defense (against the Soviet juggernaut!)
- Warsaw Pact (1955) – In response to NATO, the Soviet Union forms (forces!) a defensive alliance with its Eastern European neighbors

The Korean War (1950 – 1953) – sometimes referred to as "The Forgotten War"
- Communist North Korea invades Democratic South Korea
- U.N. forces (mostly U.S.) push the N. Koreans back almost to China; therefore China gets involved and pushes the U.N. forces back
- Reaches a stalemate near the 38th parallel
- Douglas MacArthur wanted to use nuclear weapons against the Chinese, and publically criticizes Truman's decisions and is therefore removed from command
- Eisenhower is elected and brings the war to an end, but it's really just a ceasefire; peace is never official. The Demilitarized Zone (DMZ) is established along the 38th parallel.

Dwight Eisenhower (1952 – 1960) (Republican)
- Personable, "grandfatherly"
- Highway Act (1956) – created the interstate highway system – essential infrastructure to support booming American economy (also good for moving around in case of nuclear attack!)

- Suez Crisis (1956) – Egypt nationalizes (takes over for Egypt) the Suez Canal (from the British and French who controlled it)
  - Britain and France threaten to send troops
  - The Soviet Union threatens to intervene on behalf of Egypt
  - The U.S. gets Britain and France to back down to avoid war with the Soviets
  - Eisenhower Doctrine – the U.S. promises to help Middle Eastern countries threatened by communism (it's like the Truman Doctrine but specific to the Middle East)
- Sputnik (1957) – the first artificial satellite launched into space…and the Soviets did it first! This suggested that the Soviets were more advanced and if they could launch satellites, they could launch nuclear missiles. Thus, America faced a "missile gap." It spurred on more spending in math/science to generate better scientists in America. It also marked the beginning of the Space Race.
  - Personal note: my father shared with me his memory of going as a teenager from his home in England in 1958 to Belgium to visit the World Fair (Expo). There he saw the Soviet exhibit which showed a display of Sputnik and Soviet missile and space prowess. The American exhibit and latest technology? Color t.v.! It was actually quite amazing and exciting he said, but you can imagine that missiles beat color t.v. every time. You can see that already, though, America was preparing to lead in the couch potato industry!
  - The USSR leads the Space Race in the early 60s, but the U.S. catches up eventually and is the first to land men on the moon: Apollo 11 with Neil Armstrong and "Buzz" Aldrin.
- Secretary of State, John Dulles and the "New Look" policy
  - Less dependence on a traditional army; more airpower and nuclear bombs
  - Massive retaliation – the idea that with lots of planes and nukes, no other power should mess with the U.S. because they will "massively retaliate." However, this proves impractical; it's overkill if problems with other country are minor. What is the U.S. going to do, nuke 'em over small things? Leads to a more "flexible response" under JFK.
  - M.A.D. – mutually assured destruction – if both sides use nukes, both die. Therefore, each nuclear armed side threatens to go all the way (brinksmanship) but don't actually do it (see the Cuban Missile Crisis below).
  - Eventually, ICBMs (Intercontinental ballistic missiles) are developed so there is less of a need for planes to deliver the bombs
- U-2 Spy plane Incident (1960) – Gary Powers was shot down over the Soviet Union
  - The Soviets recovered the plane and used it as evidence that the U.S. was spying. The event caused conflict between Eisenhower and Soviet leader, Nikita Khrushchev, at a summit of that year.
- Eisenhower's farewell speech: warns about the development of the "military industrial complex" or military based economy, since it provides a reason to keep the threat of war continuing

John F. Kennedy (1960 – 1963; assassinated) (Democrat)
- 1960 election vs. Nixon – first televised debates; people who watched thought that JFK won the debate; people who listened to the debate on the radio thought Nixon won. Demonstrates the significance of appearance in politics with the new t.v. technology.
- "New Frontier" – JFK's plan for the economy; much of it failed or was watered down because he had to compromise with Southern Democrats (Dixiecrats)

- The Berlin Wall (began construction 1961)
  - It was designed to keep in the many defectors who were leaving to W. Berlin and the West because of the misery under communism
  - Became a symbol of the oppression of communism
  - Finally torn down in 1989

Cuba
- Fidel Castro had taken over and brought communism to Cuba in 1959
- Bay of Pigs Fiasco (1961)
  - The CIA trained Cuban exiles to go back to Cuba to overthrow Castro
  - The U.S. does not provide airstrikes when the exiles land at the Bay of Pigs (too much an act of war) and the exiles are easily defeated and captured
  - Major embarrassment for Kennedy and the U.S.
  - The results is a lot of distrust of America by Cuba
- Cuban Missile Crisis (October 1962)
  - U-2 spy photos reveal Soviet missile launchers in Cuba
  - The USSR is planning on putting nukes in Cuba, only 90 miles from Florida where missiles could reach all across the U.S; no evidence the nukes are there yet
  - The U.S. quarantines (blockades) Cuba, preventing the USSR from delivering the nukes; the Soviets vow to go through the blockade…the world is on the verge of nuclear war! (good example of brinkmanship) (see the movie Blast from the Past)
  - It's resolved when the Soviets remove the launchers; the U.S. removes missiles in Turkey
- For the rest of the Cold War, see the Vietnam War and 70s and 80s
- JFK's assassination (November 22, 1963)
  - Killed in Dallas by Lee Harvey Oswald
  - The Warren Commission investigation concludes he was the lone gunman
  - Many conspiracy theories persist to this day

17. The Civil Rights Era (1950ish to 1968)
- Jackie Robinson (1947) – 1st African-American player to play in Major League Baseball
- Truman desegregated the armed forces (1948)
  - The beginning of the federal gov't taking steps for civil rights
  - It angered Southern Democrats; they became the Dixiecrats, opposing such moves
- Emmett Till (1954) – 14 year old African American boy goes to Mississippi from Chicago and is lynched for saying "bye baby" or whistling at a white woman. The two white men accused are found not guilty. Shocking story and his funeral picture make national headlines.
- *Brown v. Board of Education of Topeka, Kansas* (1954)
  - Argued by the NAACP and led by Thurgood Marshall (eventually the 1st black Supreme Ct. Justice)
  - The case concluded that "separate but equal" was inherently unequal as the "separate" portion denoted a sense of inferiority by default
  - It overturned *Plessy v. Ferguson*
  - It was implemented very gradually because of southern resistance; some whites sent their kids to private schools as a result
  - After *Marbury v. Madison*, it's probably the most important Sup. Ct. case you should know

- Montgomery Bus Boycott (1955)
  - Sparked when Rosa Parks refused to give up her seat on a bus to a white man and is subsequently arrested
  - A bus boycott is organized; people walked/carpooled; the busses continue running for nearly a year, often quite empty, thus causing the company to lose money; eventually the bus company capitulates (gives in)
  - This event gives rise to Martin Luther King Jr. who helps to organize the boycott
- Little Rock Nine @ Central High School in Arkansas (1957)
  - Governor Orval Faubus disobeyed school integration requirements by using state troops (Arkansas National Guard) to prevent nine black students from getting to the school
  - Eisenhower is forced to call in the federal troops (101st Airborne) to protect the students (power play between the federal and state gov't!)

Civil Rights groups
- SCLC – Southern Christian Leadership Conference
  - Organized through churches; used boycotts, marches, etc. to achieve equality
  - Martin Luther King was the first President; this was his major organization
- SNCC ("snick") – Student Nonviolent Coordinating Committee
  - Young people getting organized for protests, voter registrations, etc (Freedom Rides, sit-ins, March on Washington, Freedom Summer, etc.)
  - It would have training to prepare for violence against them
  - Sometimes the young of SNCC (along with CORE) were frustrated by the SCLC's slower approaches and demanded more aggressive (but still nonviolent) methods
  - By the mid-late 60s, it became more radical, leaning towards the Black Power movement
- CORE – Congress of Racial Equality
  - Started during WWII, it was very similar to SNCC (participated in all the above)
- National Urban League – did much of the same above, especially in urban/city areas
- NAACP – founded in 1909 by W.E.B. DuBois, it fought against discrimination primarily in the courts (through legal means)

- Martin Luther King
  - Gained prominence because of the 1955 Montgomery Bus Boycott
  - Advocated nonviolent resistance; ideas from Gandhi and Henry David Thoreau
  - He wrote "Letter from a Birmingham Jail" in which he defended his nonviolent resistance: some whites say the timing just isn't right for integration, that blacks just need to wait…their "wait" almost always means "never"

- Greensboro Sit-ins (1960)
  - 4 black college students refuse to give up their seats at a Woolworth's lunch counter; after 6 months of subsequent sit-ins Greensboro facilities relented. Other sit-ins elsewhere ensued.
  - The goal is to nonviolently demand service; the effect is the business loses money because of the disturbance it causes and hopefully eventually gives in
- Freedom Riders (1961)
  - Black and white young people board busses and ride them through the South to see if they are served and not segregated at various public places

- o The result is eventual violence; one bus is smoke-bombed and people are beaten up
- o At the end, in Mississippi, many are arrested and forced into a brutal work camp until they are eventually released
- James Meredith (1962)
  - o Meredith attempted to go to the University of Mississippi (a.k.a. "Ole Miss")
  - o JFK had to send in federal marshals to escort him and still there was violence resulting in two deaths (sort of the university level version of the Little Rock 9)
- Birmingham movement (1963)
  - o Known as one of the most segregated cities in the country, MLK and others felt if they could end segregation here, they could end it anywhere. So they mobilized huge protests, marches, sit-ins, etc.
  - o Nicknamed "Bombingham" for all the bombs set off by whites in backlashes
    - The worst example: the 16th Street Baptist Church, where a bomb killed 4 little girls
  - o Police brutality with dogs, hoses, and the like was common
- March on Washington (1963)
  - o MLK gives his famous "I have a dream" speech
  - o "...where little black boys and black girls will be able to join hands with little white boys and white girls and walk together as sisters and brothers"
  - o "When we let freedom ring...we will be able to speed up that day when all of God's children, black men and white men, Jews and Gentile, Protestants and Catholics, will be able to join hands and sing the words of the old Negro spiritual, "Free at last! Free at last! Thank God Almighty, we are free at last!"

After JFK's assassination, LBJ's Presidency...

Lyndon Baines Johnson (1963 – 1968) (Democrat)
- He was able to accomplish much of what JFK failed to do
- The "Great Society" – declares war on poverty
  - o Major government expansion to fight poverty
  - o Creates Medicare – medical care for the elderly
  - o Creates Medicaid – medical care for low-income
  - o Headstart – federal money for poor children to go to pre-school
  - o Many other progressive legislative pieces, much of which we have today; however, the unpopularity and price tag of the Vietnam War prevented the Great Society from achieving everything LBJ hoped for
- Civil Rights Act of 1964 – LANDMARK legislation
  - o Federal laws that made it illegal to discriminate in jobs, facilities, and other important areas of everyday life. Established penalties and agencies to investigate.
  - o The official, or at least legal, end of Jim Crow
- 24th amendment passed (1964) – made poll taxes illegal (can't be made to pay to vote)
- Freedom Summer (1964)
  - o A movement of civil rights workers attempting to register blacks in the South to vote, especially in Mississippi
  - o 3 workers (2 white, 1 black) go missing and are found to be murdered. The FBI investigates and the federal gov't gets even more involved in Civil Rights
- Selma March (1965)
  - o A march in Alabama in response to the intimidation of voters; state troops attack and beat the marchers, shocking the nation while they watch it unfold

- Voting Rights Act of 1965
  - The Federal gov't guaranteed protection for blacks in voting; helped dramatically increase the number of blacks registered to vote (remember, voting = power)

Black Nationalism, Power, and Radicalism
- Despite the victories listed above, by 1965 many blacks were frustrated and fed up with the lack and pace of change. Many became increasingly radical and were willing to go beyond MLK's nonviolent means.
- Watts riots (1965)
  - Several days of riots in Los Angeles; dozens killed
- Malcolm X
  - Part of the Nation of Islam (NOI); he believed in black nationalism, that is, in creating a separate society for blacks. Believed that violence, if justified, was ok.
  - During the last year in his life, after a pilgrimage to Mecca in which he saw many races of Muslims, he started to change his views: maybe the races could work together…
  - As a result of this "softness," he was assassinated by some of his own followers
  - Paraphrase X quote: "whites used to think MLK was radical, but then Malcolm X came along, and now the whites thank the Lord for MLK!" (i.e., at least MLK is nonviolent)
- Muhammad Ali
  - One of the most famous boxers of all time; heavy weight champion
  - Also a Black Muslim (mix of Islam and black nationalism; see NOI above)
- The Black Panthers
  - Organized and militant, they advocated the use of violence and separation against and from white society. They felt that justice would never be gained from whites so they must take it into their own hands.
  - Huey Newton and Bobby Seale – two most significant leaders
  - It was not all about violence; they had a 10 point program that demanded quality housing, education, food programs, etc.
- MLK assassination (April 1968)
  - Killed by James Earl Ray
  - This is generally the marking point of the end of the modern Civil Rights Movement

18. The Vietnam War
- Prior to 1954, Vietnam was imperialized and dominated by the French (Japan in WWII)
- In 1954, Ho Chi Minh, and his communist followers, overthrew the French fortress of Dien Bien Phu, and forced the French out of Vietnam

Part 1: before major U.S. troop involvement (1954 – 1964)
- Geneva summit (1955) – Vietnam is split into communist north and non-commie South (along the 17th parallel), with an agreement to have elections to reunite the country in two years (sound familiar? Like Korea!)
- Domino theory – idea that if one Southeast nation fell to communism, then all the others would as well (extension of containment theory). It becomes the driving policy for much of the events below…
- The U.S. supported Ngo Dinh Diem, but as a Catholic and a person who didn't suffer under the French (he was living in the West), he was widely disliked by the Vietnamese

populace. He ruled as a dictator, leading monks to burn themselves in protest. He's assassinated when the U.S. withdraws their support.

- When the elections near, they are canceled because the U.S. is afraid the Vietnamese people will choose communism (ironic: the U.S. prevents democracy)
- Up to 1964, the U.S. had only "advisors" in Vietnam – troops to train the S. Vietnamese
- The North invades the South and the U.S. fears that S. Vietnam will fall (domino theory)
- Gulf of Tonkin incident (1964) – U.S. ships are apparently attacked in the Gulf of Tonkin by North Vietnamese forces
- Gulf of Tonkin Resolution – Congress authorized the president to do whatever was necessary to prevent the domino theory (essentially giving the President a "blank check")
  - o Important: the Resolution was not an act of war; later, Congress would regret giving the President so much power (See the War Powers Act of 1973)
- The result was a gradual escalation of the war, eventually involving hundreds of thousands of U.S. soldiers

Part 2: the war is on in Vietnam (1964 – 1973)
- Viet Cong – communist guerilla fighters; difficult to fight against as they knew the jungle well; plus it was hard for American GIs to know which Vietnamese were friend or foe
- Tet Offensive (1968)
  - o Tet is the Chinese (and Vietnamese) New Year – supposed to be a ceasefire
  - o N. Vietnamese forces led surprise attacks instead, and almost captured the American embassy in Saigon (capital of S. Vietnam)
  - o U.S. forces rebuff the attacks, so technically it's a victory
  - o However, watching news reports about it on t.v., the American public began to increasingly question the reasons for being in Vietnam
  - o The Tet Offensive and 1968 mark a major shift and the beginning of the downturn of the war for America
- My Lai Massacre (1968) – U.S. soldiers massacre 400+ villagers, including women and children; only stopped by an intervening helicopter full of other soldiers

Part 2 and 1/2: what's happening back in America
- Hawks vs. doves: the use of these terms is often used to describe the polarization between supporters and protestors of the war
- Soldiers' lives are often seen as a waste; no victory parades for returning soldiers like there was in WWII; in fact, soldiers were sometimes harassed for their participation in this "unjust war"
- The draft was enacted – many "dodged" the draft by fleeing to Canada or getting a deferment to go to college (thus it once again became a blue collar fight)
- LBJ becomes very unpopular because of the Vietnam War failures
  - o He announces he will not run for President in 1968
- 1968 Election
  - o Democrats split between Eugene McCarthy (the peace guy), Bobby Kennedy (RFK), and Hubert Humphrey (LBJ's VP who is seen as the same as LBJ)
  - o Bobby Kennedy is assassinated while running for the Democratic nomination
  - o The Southern Democrat vote is further split by George Wallace running on the American Independent Party;
    - ▪ "Segregation now, segregation tomorrow, segregation forever!"
  - o The 1968 Democratic Convention in Chicago – protestors interacted violently with police as frustration over the election and the war boiled over (fiasco!)

- o Republicans nominate Richard Nixon and he wins
  - The late 60s become, for some, a mix of war protests and counterculture (drugs, hippies, music [Bob Dylan, Jimi Hendrix, Woodstock festival])
  - Kent State [college in Ohio] (1970) – at Kent State, student protestors are fired upon by the National Guard; 4 students are killed. Our own troops firing upon our own people?! What's happening with this #$%#$ war? – that's what some people were thinking and how far many had lost faith in the war.

Part 3: Nixon and the end of the war (1968 to 1973-75)
- Vietnamization – the process of withdrawing American troops and giving more responsibility to the South Vietnamese forces; American forces gradually pull out...
- Ho Chi Minh Trail – a pathway that the Viet Cong use to supply guerilla fighters in S. Vietnam that goes through the jungles of Cambodia and Laos
  - o Nixon orders the secret bombing of Cambodia to slow this supply trail but it is found out and angers the doves (we're not at war with Cambodia and Laos); also seen as further abuse and secrecy by the gov't and President in particular
- Despite the large protests, Nixon insisted there was a "silent majority" who supported him
- 1973 – Paris Peace Accords – The U.S. pulls out of Vietnam, leaving behind S. Vietnam to fend for itself (many S. Vietnamese desperately try to go with Americans...)
- Fall of Saigon (1975) – The South holds out for 2 years but eventually loses. Vietnam is united under communism (still to this day). Cambodia later falls to communism (domino theory proves at least somewhat true).
- Conclusion:
  - o 26th amendment passed – reduces the legal voting age to 18; if young men at 18 were old enough to be drafted and die for our country, they're old enough to vote
  - o In the end, the U.S. lost the will to fight whereas the fighting peasants of Vietnam did not give in, outlasting the might of the American military
  - o 58,000 + U.S. soldiers KIA and MIA
  - o Literally millions of North and South Vietnamese, soldiers and civilians died
  - o Many Vietnamese flee Vietnam and emigrate to the U.S.
    - ▪ The so-called "boat people" term is derived because a number actually get on boats and flee the country, sometimes dying in the dangerous process

19. The 1970s (off the hook!)
Richard Nixon (1968 – 1974 resigned) (Republican)
- Détente – relaxed tensions with the Soviet Union
  - o SALT – Strategic Arms Limitation Talks – gradual reduction of nuclear missiles (although there were still enough to annihilate each other)
  - o Nixon visited China in 1972; helped to ease tensions there and helped put pressure on the Soviets to compromise (they were often at odds with China)
- 70s economy
  - o Stagflation (stagnating/slow economy + inflation [rising prices]) during the 70s
  - o 1973 and 1979 oil crises
    - ▪ One reason was because OPEC (Organization of Petroleum Exporting Countries) embargoed oil sales to the U.S. because America supported Israel in the 1967 and 1973 Israel-Arab conflicts in the Middle East
- 1972 – Bobby Fischer defeats Boris Spassky in the World Chess Championship

- More than just a chess match, it was the Cold War being played out on 64 squares!!
- Environmental Protection Agency (EPA) is formed under Nixon
- War Powers Act (1973) – as a reaction to the Vietnam War and a fear of it happening again, Congress limited the President to deploying troops for 60 days in a conflict; after that, the President needed Congressional approval or the troops had to be removed

Watergate Scandal (1972 – 1973) (way to go Forrest Gump!)

- Pre-Gate – Daniel Ellsberg, a reporter, leaked the Pentagon Papers, documents that revealed the ineptitude, deceitfulness, and corrupt decision making of the U.S. gov't in the war in Vietnam
    - Nixon became obsessed with stopping such leaks so he got some "plumbers" (security agents) to investigate and intimidate various people (using illegal methods at times). They actually broke into Ellsberg's psychiatrist's office to find things to blackmail him with.
- The Watergate is a hotel; Democrats had their national headquarters there in an office
- The office was burglarized (some bugs were planted); eventually the burglary was linked to members of CREEP (the Committee to re-elect the President)
- Gradually, evidence of "hush – money" and rumors begin to indicate the White House was involved
- Washington Post reporters and "Deep Throat" contact reveal that Nixon has secretly taped all his conversations in the Oval Office (at the White House). Congress demands to have the tapes to determine if there's any evidence of Nixon's involvement in the Watergate coverup.
- Meanwhile, if things weren't bad enough, Vice President Spiro Agnew resigns under tax-evasion charges (corruption everywhere!)
- Nixon claims "executive privilege" – the President doesn't need to give over the tapes
- "Saturday Night Massacre" – Nixon orders the Attorney General to fire the attorneys who are investigating him. The Attorney General resigns in protest (the name indicates people losing their jobs; no one is actually massacred!)
- Congress begins to draw up impeachment procedures for Nixon
- The tapes are finally handed over but missing parts; further tapes are eventually seized and they incriminate Nixon in obstruction of justice and a coverup
- On the verge of impeachment, Nixon resigns on Aug. 9th, 1974.
- The result: government mistrust reaches a maximum after Vietnam and now Watergate

Gerald Ford (1974 – 1976) (Republican)

- He is mostly known for pardoning Richard Nixon. As a result, Nixon never faced any punishment for Presidential scandals. Some speculated whether there was sort of deal between Nixon and Ford (the nation gets to avoid lengthy, embarrassing impeachment trial and Nixon gets to go free)

Jimmy Carter (1976 – 1980) (Democrat)

- He was unable to get much done with the poor economy and energy crises going on
- Camp David Accords – Camp David is the Presidential retreat area. There, peace was negotiated between Egypt and Israel.
- Iran – Hostage Crisis (1979)

- Back in the 50s, the U.S. had helped the Shah of Iran get into power because he promised to be anti-communist; however he was a dictator and unpopular
- In 1979, the Islamic Revolution occurred in which the people of Iran overthrew the Shah; the U.S. then let the Shah come to America for medical treatment, rather than go stand trial in Iran
- In response, Iranians took over the U.S. embassy in Iran. They held the captives for 444 days. Suffice to say, it was a major debacle.

- Soviet invasion of Afghanistan (1979) – leads to a 10 year war for the Soviets in Afghanistan (their Vietnam); the U.S. supplies weapons to the mujahedeen or freedom fighters (some turn out to be the Taliban later!) (see movie: Charlie Wilson's War)
- 1980 winter Olympics: "Miracle on Ice" – U.S. defeats the highly rated Soviet ice hockey team in a Cold War faceoff (literally and figuratively!)

20. 1980s (that's radical; totally cool; don't gag me with a spoon!)

Ronald Reagan (1980 – 1988) (Republican) – famous for eating his jelly beans!
- He represents the resurgence of conservatism
- Conservative groups or names: the New Right, Moral Majority, Christian Coalition
  - A reaction or backlash to the liberal aspects of the 60s and the economic/gov't direction since the New Deal
  - The idea is that the hippies, the liberal morals, and all such things, led to a moral degradation in society while the government has gotten too big and expensive
- "Government is not the solution to our problem, government is the problem!"
  - Goal was to reduce the size of gov't; cut taxes
  - Supply – side economics (a.k.a. "trickle – down" economics) (a.k.a. "Reaganomics")
    - Cut taxes and the money saved by the rich will "trickle – down" to the lower segments of society. Result: a growing gap between rich and poor.
  - Unfortunately, taxes were cut but defense spending (because of the Cold War arms race) was expanded; lower taxes + higher spending = deficit spending and debt. Result: a major increase in the national debt. This problem has only gotten worse in the last 30 years as the U.S. continues to spend more than it takes in via taxes.
  - This debate between conservatives who want smaller gov't and liberals who believe a large gov't is necessary to support/protect people is still raging on today
- Election of 1984 – Reagan wins in a landslide
- Iran – Contra Affair (Scandal) (1986)
  - The U.S. (secretly) sold weapons to Iran to free some hostages and then turned around and used the money to fund the Contras, an anti-communist guerilla group in Nicaragua, who were fighting the communists there (Sandinistas).
  - This was scandalous because the gov't wasn't supposed to be doing either of these secret/shady deals
  - Colonel Oliver North became the fall guy (scapegoat)
  - Like Watergate, the question became: how much did the President know about this? In the end, little of the scandal stuck to Reagan (the "Teflon President").
- Space Shuttle Challenger Disaster (1986) – the shuttle blows up within minutes of launch. A national tragedy; included in the dead astronauts was a school teacher.

- AIDS epidemic (Acquired Immune Deficiency Syndrome) – the disease was really made public during the 1980s and was highly stigmatized in the early years; the past 30 years has seen a major public effort to combat it and its effects.
- Cold War continued…
  - As above, the U.S. increased defense spending; essentially the U.S. "outspent the Soviets" to win the war
  - Strategic Defense Initiative (SDI or "Star Wars") – Idea of using lasers in space to shoot down any Soviet nuclear missiles (a "defense shield") – not really feasible but it caused the Soviets to spend a lot of money in response
  - Mikhail Gorbachev – The Soviet leader during much of the 80s. He tried to reform the Soviet Union. Two important related terms:
    - Glasnost – "openness" – an attempt to reduce restrictions under communism; give the people more freedoms
    - Perestroika – "restructuring" – a freeing up of the command economy under communism
  - Despite these attempts to "save" communism by giving the people more choice, the reaction in Eastern Europe was to throw off the bonds of communism
    - The result was the fall of the Berlin Wall and collapse of communism in Eastern Europe (Nov 1989) – Germany reunited within one year
  - Next the Soviet Union itself collapsed in 1991. Today, the USSR does not exist; it is now Russia and various neighbors instead.

21. 1990s to the present

George Bush (1988 – 1992)

- See the above end of Cold War as it technically happens during his Presidency.
- Tiananmen Square Massacre (1989) – Chinese gov't massacres freedom/rights protesters
- Bush made a campaign promise: "Read my lips, no new taxes"
  - Subsequently, as part of a compromise with Congress, he raised taxes
  - This proves to be a major reason for him not getting re-elected
- Persian Gulf War (1st War in Iraq) (1990 – 1991)
  - Saddam Hussein of Iraq invades neighboring Kuwait
  - The U.S. defeats Iraq in the name of democracy for Kuwait (but cynically also because Kuwait and the region are major oil suppliers [keep regional stability!])
    - Known as Operation Desert Storm (General Colin Powell gains fame)
  - American technology (smart bombs, etc.) led to a quick American victory
  - Hussein was allowed to stay in power, which becomes a problem later

Bill Clinton (1992 – 2000) (Democrat)

- The election of 1992 featured a 3rd person running, Ross Perot, a Texas billionaire, running as an independent
- NAFTA (North American Free Trade Agreement) passed – reduced tariffs and competition between the U.S., Canada, and Mexico
- Much of the 90s proved to be good, economically, so Clinton benefited from that
- 1991 – Rodney King beating – King was a black man whose beating by policemen was caught on video. Police officers were found not guilty; resulted in major riots in L.A.
- Monica Lewinsky scandal – Clinton had an affair with Lewinsky, a White House intern, and it led to his impeachment (guilty of perjury but was found not guilty of high crimes and misdemeanors which is what they need to remove the Pres.)

George W. Bush (2000 – 2008) (Republican)
- 2000 election Bush vs. Al Gore
  - *Bush v. Gore* – The election resulted in such a close vote, it came down to the state of Florida. However, there were disputed votes in the state and the decision of which votes to use or not could change the election. This Supreme Ct. case helped resolve the issue and the result was a victory for Bush.
- September 11, 2001 – Terrorist attacks on the World Trade Center and Pentagon.
  - Four planes were hijacked by Al Qaeda terrorists. Two strike the two towers of the World Trade Center, another hits the Pentagon (Department of Defense main building) and the 4th crashes in a field (likely it would have gone for the White House or Capitol Building).
  - Sparks the War on Terror
  - The U.S. invades Afghanistan (Oct. 2001) and still has troops there
  - The U.S. invades Iraq (2003) suspecting that they have weapons of mass destruction
    - Subsequent occupation lasts until 2011
  - Hurricane Katrina (2005)

Barack Obama (2008 – ?) (Democrat)
- First African American elected President
- 2008 Financial Crisis which leads to global economic problems through 2012
- Healthcare reform (2010) – President Obama succeeds in passing major reforms to healthcare which prove to be controversial

Expansion

Land Addition	Significance
Louisiana Purchase (1803)	$15 million dollars; bought by Thomas Jefferson from France/Napoleon Doubled the size of the United States Jefferson, with his strict constructionist views, hesitated in buying it since the Constitution did not expressly permit it, but did so anyway since it was such a good deal
Florida (1819)	Adams-Onis Treaty with Spain Gave the U.S. control of Florida and set the boundary between the LA Purchase and Spanish territory The U.S. surrendered claims in TX to Spain
Maine Dispute (1842)	Fighting erupted between some feisty lumberjacks (called the Aroostook War) in disputed territory in Maine between the U.S. and British held Canada The British got a Halifax-Quebec road they wanted and both sides got some of the land, thus avoiding any considerable hostilities
Texas Annexation (1845)	After TX had been an independent republic for 9 years, it was annexed or added onto the United States (Mexico did not agree…)
Oregon (1846)	Some Americans wanted more of the Oregon territory to 54° 40″ (54° 40″ or fight!); the British wanted the border settled much further south A compromise was reached along the 49th parallel (present day border), thus preventing war with England The U.S. now stretched from sea to sea (access to the Pacific)
Mexican Cession (1848)	Acquired in the Treaty of Guadalupe – Hidalgo (Who wants to party!?) The U.S. paid $15 million and acquired California and large portions of the Southwest Led to conflict over status of slavery in territory won from Mexico Wilmot Proviso (1846) would have banned slavery in any captured territory but it failed to pass in Congress
Gadsden Purchase (1853)	Southerners hoped to build the first continental railroad but the mountains of northern Arizona/New Mexico would have made it difficult. Therefore, the U.S. purchased land from Mexico south of the mountains that was more level. In the end, however, the South failed to get the RR first. $10 million (Criticized for being $10 million for cactus/tumbleweed)
Cuba (failed attempt, 1854)	Spain refused $100 million for purchase of Cuba Three American envoys meet and form a plan (manifesto) to offer $120 million and hint at a take over if that fails The plan goes public and angers northerners at secret southern expansionist plots
Nicaragua (failed attempt, 1856)	In an attempt to extend slavery, William Walker captured Nicaragua and legalized slavery. He was overthrown by regional powers and shot.

African American History

<u>Up to the Civil War (rise and fall of slavery) [colonial – 1865]</u>
- 1619 – 1st 20 slaves arrive in Jamestown; in early years, slaves were more expensive than indentured servants
- African slaves were particularly useful in rice cultivation (S. Carolina) since they had previous skill in this and were resistant to malaria and thus died less often
- The Royal African Company lost its charter eventually meaning any ship could transport slaves for profit and sure enough, it was profitable, leading to increased slave trade. Notably, although slavery was not as popular in New England, it was often shippers from their that often cashed in on the Transatlantic slave trade.
- By the late 1600s, wages rose in England meaning less people were willing or available to come over as indentured servants. The result was a gradual increase in the use of slaves.
- Bacon's Rebellion (1676) – frustration of poor indentured servants who upon gaining their freedom found that most of the good land was taken; the only available land was on the frontier, but that led to increasing Indian attacks; Nathanial Bacon led a rebellion against the planter class, burning Jamestown as a result and forcing the governor (Berkeley) to flee. Bacon died of disease and the rebellion collapsed but the result was less use of indentured servants and an increased use of slaves (major turning point in the history of slavery).
- Important to note: despite the eventual prevalence of slavery in the South all colonies/states had slavery early on; not until soon before and after the Revolutionary War did northern colonies/states begin to outlaw slavery
- See the rest of slavery development including, for example, the Missouri Compromise, abolitionism, and the leadup to the Civil War section to review

Attempts to solve the slavery issue by the gov't (compromises)
- 1787 – Northwest Ordinance – prohibited slavery in the Old Northwest
- 3/5 Compromise in the Constitution – how slaves were counted in representation
- 1820 – the Missouri Compromise – dealt with slavery in the LA Purchase lands
- 1846 – Wilmot Proviso – attempt to ban slavery in Mexican Cession territory
- Compromise of 1850 – attempt to balance pro- and anti-slavery views
- 1857 – *Dred Scott* decision – slaves are not citizens but property, so the gov't cannot regulate where slavery can spread since property rights are protected

<u>Post Civil-War (segregation)</u>
Reconstruction:
- Freedmen's Bureau
  - Federal gov't organization designed to help freedmen with food, clothing, medical care, and education
  - succeeded mostly in the area of education and literacy; insufficient in other areas
- Black codes
  - laws that Southern states passed to restrict freedmen / maintain control over them
- Many freedmen were reduced to <u>sharecropping</u> – working someone else's land and being required to pay with the crop you produce. Often resulted in eventual debt which became a form of economic slavery. Freedmen became contractually tied to the land.
- Rise of the Ku Klux Klan (KKK)

- o Created to scare freedmen and use violence/fear to control the black population
- o The federal government actually cracked down on the Klan and it became quite small by the end of Reconstruction and only came back into prominence later…
- Amendments passed
  - o 13th (1865) – abolishes slavery
  - o 14th (1868) – blacks given citizenship; all citizens guaranteed due process of law and equal protection of the law; federal gov't would protect rights if states failed to do so
  - o 15th (1870) – cannot be deprived the right to vote based on race or being a former slave

Frequently used ways of taking away the right to vote from blacks included:
- Literacy tests – required to be able to read to vote (but wait some whites couldn't read)
- Poll taxes – had to pay a tax to vote (but wait, some whites are too poor to vote too…)
- Grandfather clause – if your grandfather couldn't vote, then you can't either (this works: it doesn't affect whites while ensuring blacks can't vote)

Jim Crow era
- Jim Crow laws – laws that enforced segregation; lynching common
- 1896 *Plessy v. Ferguson* – case that established *separate but equal* – legalized segregation!
- Sharecropping kept blacks tied to the land; an economic slavery or servitude

Booker T. Washington (Wait) Vs.	W.E.B. DuBois (Demand)
Economic equality	Political/social equality
Work hard and earn whites' respect	Demand equality
Industrial/vocational training (use hands)	Higher education
Founded Tuskegee Institute	1st black Phd Harvard graduate
	Founded NAACP
	Wanted to develop the "talented tenth"

- "BTW wants to make men into carpenters; I [Dubois] want to turn carpenters into men!"
- Ida B. Wells – Afr. Am. woman who successfully led a crusade against lynchings

1920s - Marcus Garvey – African American leader who promoted black self-sufficiency (shop at black owned businesses) and the "Back to Africa" movement
- o Created the Universal Negro Improvement Association (UNIA)
- o Had his own Black Star line of shipping to take blacks back to Africa
- o Significant black leader between the eras of DuBois/Washington and MLK/Malcolm X
- o In the end, he was arrested for fraud and deported

African Americans in WWII
- o Great Migration – African Americans moved to the north in record numbers finding war jobs in major cities (as often is the case, this led to racial tension)
- o A. Philip Randolph – threatened a march on Washington D.C. because of discrimination; FDR created the Fair Employment Practices Commission to help satisfy him
- o Blacks still had to serve in segregated units in the military
- o Tuskegee airmen – famous group of black aviators (pilots)

<u>Civil Rights Era (1950-1968)</u>

- Martin Luther King
  - Gained prominence because of the 1955 Montgomery Bus Boycott
  - Advocated nonviolent resistance; ideas from Gandhi and Henry David Thoreau
  - Wrote "Letter from a Birmingham Jail" in which he defended his nonviolent resistance: some whites say the timing just isn't right for integration, that blacks just need to wait...their "wait" almost always means "never"
- Malcolm X
  - Part of the Nation of Islam (NOI); believed in black nationalism, that is, in creating a separate society for blacks. Believed that violence, if justified, was ok.
  - During the last year in his life, after a pilgrimage to Mecca in which he saw many races of Muslims, he started to change his views: maybe the races could work together...
  - As a result of this "softness," he was assassinated by some of his own followers
  - Paraphrase X quote: "whites used to think MLK was radical, but then Malcolm X came along, and now the whites thank the Lord for MLK!" (i.e., at least he's nonviolent)
- Thurgood Marshall becomes the first black Supreme Court Justice

<u>Since 1968</u>

- Shirley Chisholm – the first African American woman elected to Congress in 1968

Native American History

<u>Pre – Colonial Era</u>
- Native Americans are believed to have come across a land bridge connecting Asia and Alaska was exposed around 10,000 B.C. during an ice age
- In North America: very diverse; tended to be hunter-gatherers and subsistent farmers; few large, well-developed civilizations
- Respect for nature as compared to Europeans who saw nature as something to be conquered. Europeans saw Indians as lazy because they weren't "harnessing" the land.
- A majority of early native populations died from diseases brought by Europeans which the natives did not have immunities to (e.g. smallpox)

<u>Colonial conflicts:</u>
- 1680 – <u>Pueblo Revolt</u> (Pope's Rebellion) [against the Spanish]
  - Natives in the Southwest rebel against the Spanish and succeed in destroying churches and pushing the Spanish out for about 10 years. Then Pope, the leader, dies and the Spanish return.
- <u>Anglo-Powhatan Wars</u> – conflicts with local Indians near Jamestown (Pocahontas's tribe)
- <u>Pequot War</u> (1636) – English Puritan colonists massacre natives
- <u>King Philip's War</u> (1676) – natives attack villages along the frontier; massacre many settlers. However, the next year the English settlers attack and push the natives further back (Lesson: native rebellions rarely work).
- <u>Pontiacs Rebellion in 1763</u> – Native Am. leader Pontiac unites tribes in the Ohio valley and attacks Ft. Detroit and attempts to push American colonists back east. Result is: the Proclamation of 1763.

- French and Indian War and the War of 1812 – significance as far as Native Americans is that in both wars the natives are used as pawns between the two powers at war

<u>1830s</u>
- 1830 – Congress passes the <u>Indian Removal Act</u> – forced natives from the Southeast (Georgia, Florida, etc.), including the "5 Civilized Tribes" to the west of the Mississippi (Oklahoma primarily)
- Trail of Tears (1837) – thousands of Cherokee are relocated to Oklahoma; 4,000 die on the way. A result of Jackson's Indian policy and 1830 Removal Act (see above).

<u>Post – Civil War</u>
- Great Plains Indians were the most notable group during the Gilded Age
- Dependent on the vast herds of buffalo; they used them for food, shelter, clothing…
  - The U.S. army recognized that the best way to wipe out the Indian, was to wipe out the buffalo. Millions of buffalo eventually dwindled to several thousand.
- From 1850 to 1890, tribes were systematically forced onto reservations (usually the poorest, left over land)
- Children were often taken from their parents and forced to assimilate
- Dawes Severalty Act (1887)
  - Broke up tribal reservation land into individual family plots (160 acres) – sort of a Homestead Act for Indians
  - It was an attempt to assimilate the natives; make them more like white farmers

- To make things worse, whites would often come later and swindle the individual, unsuspecting Indians out of their already low-quality land
- Helen Hunt Jackson wrote a book called "A Century of Dishonor" in 1881, which discussed the long history of injustices of the U.S. gov't toward Native Americans, such as the many broken treaties they had made…
- Key Battles
  - 1864 – Sand Creek Massacre – despite an American flag and a peace medal given them by President Lincoln, Black Kettle and White Antelope and their Cheyenne followers were massacred by Colonel Chivington and the U.S. army in Colorado
  - 1876 – Battle of Little Bighorn
    - After gold was discovered in the Black Hills of the Dakota territory (and within the Sioux reservation), gold seekers flood the area leading to conflict
    - This led to a huge gathering of natives in nearby Montana. There Colonel Custer and his 264 men stumbled into thousands of native warriors and were massacred. A rare and short-lived victory for Native Americans.
  - 1890 – Massacre at Wounded Knee
    - As U.S. soldiers were disarming some Sioux Indians, a shot rang out and the soldiers began shooting into the crowd of Indians, massacring 128 men, women, and children
    - This was the last major Indian conflict…few major events after this
- The 1890 census is seen as the close of the Frontier; no more line between civilization and non; the West is broken up with settlements

1930s

- Indian Reorganization Act of 1934 – (Indian "New Deal") – a shift from assimilation to providing autonomy for tribes, etc. (overall an improvement)

1970s

- American Indian Movement (AIM) of the 1970s
  - Native Americans take over Alcatraz
  - Clash with federal agents at Wounded Knee in 1973 (site of the 1890 massacre)
- Reservations today often have high rates of alcoholism, unemployment, and poverty
  - Some have turned to gambling casinos to make money to support the tribe

History of Women in the United States

<u>Colonial Era</u>
- Republican motherhood - women's responsibility to raise virtuous children who would continue the legacy of republican values (loyalty, honesty, freedom, etc.)

<u>In the mid and late 1800s</u>
- "Cult of domesticity" – glorified the role of women as homemaker; raise children
  - Part of this was a result that traditional work for women by this time was decreasing; all family members in the home used to contribute but now the work was increasingly in factories and not "cottage industries." It became a social status and expectation that women at home do less "work" and more traditional homemaking (which it turns out can be quite a bit of work!).
- Women were very much involved in the 2nd great awakening (empowered women's desire for more rights)
- Early – mid 1800s – women become important in teaching and the rise of women's colleges
- Women could not vote; many lost their property when they got married
- Lucretia Mott – famous women's right advocate; angered when women were excluded from the World's Anti-Slavery Convention in 1840; she helped organize the Seneca Falls Convention (with Elizabeth Cady Stanton)
- Lucy Stone – educated women's rights crusader; retained her maiden name after marriage
- Elizabeth Blackwell – first woman to receive a medical degree
- 1848 – <u>Seneca Falls Convention</u>: Leading women met and drew up the <u>Declaration of Sentiments</u> ("…that all men <u>and</u> women are created equal…") (Note: Susan B. Anthony was not at Seneca Falls)
- Susan B. Anthony and Elizabeth Cady Stanton founded the National Woman Suffrage Association (1869) advocating for women's rights including suffrage (right to vote)
- Western, frontier states were the first to grant women suffrage (Wyoming 1st in 1869)
- Amelia Bloomer and Margaret Fuller also noteworthy early female leaders

<u>Women's Suffrage attempts in the Progressive Era and 1920s</u>
- National American Woman Suffrage Association (NAWSA) – Carrie Chapman Catt
- National Woman's Party (NWP) – more radical – Alice Paul
  - Gave Wilson grief during the war, advocating that "Kaiser Wilson" should enfranchise women
- 19th amendment (1920) – granted women's suffrage
- Margaret Sanger (1920s) – advocated use of birth control – quite radical for the time; argued that women were enslaved to men because of the cycle of pregnancy and childrearing
- Flappers (1920s) – women who challenged traditional expectations – they cut their hair, smoked, drank, wore shorter skirts (Hello! Check out that ankle!!)

<u>1950s</u>
- Women were expected to be married and take of her home, husband, and children; a new "Cult of domesticity" developed
  - Rebellion to this gradually developed; rise of feminism and the sexual revolution of the late 60s

Epic U.S. History Review

- Betty Friedan – wrote a book, "The Feminine Mystique" (1963) – gave voice to women's dissatisfaction with this traditional role. "Is this all?" she asked.

<u>1970s</u>

- Equal Rights Amendment proposed (ERA) – ultimately it failed as many felt that women already had equality; why mandate it with an amendment?
  - Phyllis Schlafly – a notable conservative woman who opposed it
- Title IX (9) – mandated that women's opportunities in education not be discriminating against, most notably creating and increasing opportunities/funding in girls athletics

<u>1980s</u>

- Sandra Day O'Conner – She was the first female Supreme Court Justice

History of Immigration in the U.S.

<u>1840s – 1850s</u> the "Old Immigrants" (the first big wave)
The English, Irish, and Germans

<u>Irish</u>	<u>Germans</u>
Came to America after the potato famine in the 1840s	Came to America after the failed revolution of 1848, fleeing autocratic rule; crop failures
Settled in the Northeast cities	After arriving, tended to move to the Midwest
Came over poor and unskilled	Tended to come with more wealth and education
Catholic	More often Protestant
Competition with blacks for jobs	Lived in communities
NINA – No Irish Need Apply	Alcohol
Alcohol	
Concentrated political power in the cities (political machines)	

- Nativism (nativist) – the movement against foreigners/immigrants
- Know Nothing Party – a.k.a., the Order of the Star Spangled Banner, a nativist party in the mid 1800s

<u>Late 1800s – Era of "New Immigrants"</u> from southern/eastern Europe including: Italians, Poles, Greeks, Jews from Russia, etc.
  - o They were considerably different than "old" immigrants so they faced even more discrimination
  - o Many were willing to work for low wages; employed as "scabs" or strikebreakers. They helped build up America's industrial power.
  - o Some were "birds of passage," or those who intended to return to their country
  - o Many immigrants lived in big cities, in slums and ethnic neighborhoods [ghettos] like Chinatown, Little Italy, etc.
- Nativists opposing immigrants during this era might join the APA, American Protective Association, which wanted restrictions on immigrants
- To help immigrants with the transition, settlement houses were formed, where immigrants could get job training, English classes, child care, etc. The most famous was the Hull House in Chicago, founded by Jane Addams.

- Many Chinese immigrants came initially for the gold rush but when that dried up, many worked on the Transcontinental Railroad
- 1882 – Chinese Exclusion Act is passed – prevented immigration and restricted rights

<u>1920s</u>
- Red Scare – there was a fear of communist influence in America after the Communist Revolution in Russia (1917). Anything resembling pro-labor was considered too liberal and pro-communist (workers unite!). Thus it applied to the things below: immigrants, etc.
- *Buford* (1919) (a.k.a. the "Soviet Ark) – a ship that was sent to the USSR full of deported anarchist and pro-communist supporters
- Emergency Quota Act of 1921 – made a quota that limited the number of immigrants to 3% of how ever many were in the U.S. as of the 1910 census.

- 1924 National Origins Act – revised the quota to 2% of the 1890 census. Result: Reduced some (undesirable "New Immigrants") while keeping others (British)
- Rise of the KKK – this was the heyday of the Klan, i.e., its largest size ever with millions of members. It was supported by WASPs (White, Anglo-Saxon, Protestants) and was against anyone not like them! It declined by the late 1920s.
- A. Mitchell Palmer – Attorney General – he hunted down suspected communists
- Sacco and Vanzetti – a couple of radical Italian anarchists who were arrested for murder and electrocuted (shocking, eh?!). However, it was based on weak evidence, so most people believe they were really convicted to make an example of rejection of radical views and being immigrants (the Red Scare!).

Immigration Act of 1965 – eliminated the 1920s quotas and setup much more liberal quotas based on skills needed and relations with U.S. citizen families, etc. The result was large numbers of non-European immigrants for the first time.
   o Over the past 45 years large groups from Asian and Latin American countries have immigrated to the U.S. both legally and illegally

Top 15 Presidents and key events to associate with their Presidencies

(It really helps with timeline stuff if you keep track of important events by knowing the timeframe of important Presidents) (order is chronological, not based on importance)

1. Geroge Washington (1789 – 1796)
   - Two-term precedent
   - Neutrality proclamation (1793)
   - Put down the Whiskey Rebellion (1794)
   - Farewell Address (1796)
   - Hamilton – assumption and the Bank of the U.S.
   - Beginning of the first party system – Federalists vs. Democratic Republicans

2. John Adams (1796 – 1800)
   - XYZ Affair
   - Quasi-War with France
   - Alien and Sedition Acts
   - Virginia and Kentucky Resolutions

3. Thomas Jefferson (1800 – 1808)
   - 1800 election – peaceful transition of power
   - Louisiana Purchase
   - Lewis and Clark
   - *Marbury v. Madison* (judicial review!)
   - Chesapeake incident
   - Embargo Act (O Grab Me!)

4. Andrew Jackson (1828 – 1836)
   - "Era of the Common Man"
   - Spoils System
   - Nullification Crisis
   - Indian Removal Act of 1830
   - Bank War

5. James K. Polk (1844 – 1848)
   - Oregon boundary resolved with England
   - Mexican – American War (1846 – 1848)
     - Wilmot Proviso
     - Acquires CA

6. Abraham Lincoln (1860 – 1865)
   - Fort Sumter
   - Attempts to keep Border States in the Union
   - *Trent* Affair
   - Emancipation Proclamation
   - Gettysburg Address
   - First President assassinated

7. Theodore Roosevelt (1901 – 1908)
   - Negotiates end to the Russo-Japanese War
   - Gentleman's Agreement
   - Voyage of the Great White Fleet
   - "Big Stick" diplomacy
   - Roosevelt Corollary to the Monroe Doctrine
   - Began construction of the Panama Canal
   - Square Deal (3 C's)
   - Trustbuster
   - Anthracite coal strike (1902)
   - Muckrakers
   - Major conservation legislation

8. Woodrow Wilson (1912 – 1920)
   - Most of the Progressive amendments passed (16, 17, 18, 19)
   - Federal Reserve Act
   - Russian Revolution
   - Sinking of the *Lusitania*
   - Zimmerman Telegram
   - World War I
   - Make the "world safe for democracy" and "a war to end all wars"
   - Idealism – Fourteen Points and "Peace without victors"
   - Versailles Treaty

9. Franklin D. Roosevelt (1932 – 1945)
   - New Deal (3 R's)
     - 1st Hundred Days
     - Bank Holiday and Fireside Chats
     - AAA, CCC, FDIC, TVA, WPA
     - Social Security
     - Court-packing scheme
   - Good Neighbor Policy
   - Neutrality Acts of 1930s
   - Gradual involvement in helping Britain in WWII
     - Cash and carry
     - Bases for destroyers deal
     - Lend-Lease
     - Be the "arsenal of democracy"
   - Germany invades Poland
   - Pearl Harbor – Dec. 7th, 1941
   - A. Philip Randolph threatens a march on Washington
   - Internment of Japanese-Americans
   - Atlantic Charter, Casablanca, Tehran, and Yalta Conferences

10. Harry S Truman (1945 – 1952)
    - Dropped the atomic bombs on Hiroshima and Nagasaki
    - Truman Doctrine and containment

- Marshall Plan (1947)
- Berlin Airlift (1948 – 49)
- NATO (1949)
- 1949 China becomes communist and Soviets develop nuclear bomb
- Korean War begins (1950 – 53)
- HUAC, McCarthyism, Rosenbergs (2nd Red Scare)
- Fair Deal
- Jackie Robinson and integration of Major League Baseball
- Desegregates the armed forces (1948)

11. Dwight D. Eisenhower (1952 – 1960)
- Ended the Korean War
- Sputnik (1957)
- U-2 Spy plane incident
- *Brown v. Board of Education* (1954)
- Montgomery Bus Boycott
- Little Rock Nine
- Interstate Highway Act
- Farewell Address: Beware the "military-industrial complex"

12. John F. Kennedy (1960 – 1963)
- Berlin Wall construction begins
- Bay of Pigs (1961)
- Cuban Missile Crisis (1962)
- Assassination of Ngo Dinh Diem
- Freedom Riders
- James Meredith and the integration of Univ. of Mississippi (Ole Miss)
- Martin Luther King's March on Washington
- New Frontier
- Assassinated by Lee Harvey Oswald

13. Lyndon B. Johnson (1963 – 1968)
- Great Society
- War on Poverty
- Medicare/Medicaid
- Civil Rights Act of 1964
- 24th amendment passed (outlaws poll taxes)
- Selma March
- Voting Rights Act of 1965
- Immigration and Nationality Act of 1965
- Gulf of Tonkin
- Tet Offensive
- Assassination of MLK and Bobby Kennedy (1968)

14. Richard Nixon (1968 – 1974)
- Kent State (1970)
- Bombing of Cambodia

- Vietnamization
- Ends U.S. involvement in Vietnam war
- 26th amendment passed
- Watergate
- War Powers Act (1973)
- Détente; SALT I; visits China
- Resigns (only President to do so)

15. <u>Ronald Reagan (1980 – 1988)</u>
- Resurgence of conservatism in 1980s
- "Trickle-down" economics
- Star Wars (SDI)
- Dealings with Mikhail Gorbachev
- Iran-Contra Affair (scandal)
- AIDS epidemic begins
- Teflon President

Most Significant Amendments

Bill of Rights (1st 10 amendments approved as part of ratification of the Constitution)

- 1st – government cannot restrict freedom of religion, speech, assembly, petition, press
- 2nd – right to bear arms (guns)
- 3rd – gov't cannot quarter (or house) soldiers in people's homes (not very relevant today, but shows how big a grievance this was to the Founders)
- 4th – gov't cannot make unreasonable searches and seizures
- 5th – prohibits double jeopardy, self-incrimination ("plead the 5th"); prohibits the gov't from seizing property without "due process"
- 6th – guarantees accused criminals the right to speedy/public trial; impartial jury, etc.
- 7th – right to a trial by jury in civil cases
- 8th – no excessive bail or fines or cruel/unusual punishment (a great example of how the document evolves because of interpretation…what has been interpreted as "cruel and unusual" has changed over time…)
- 9th – these rights specifically protected in the Constitution do not mean that unlisted rights are not protected
- 10th – powers not specified to the federal gov't are reserved for the state/people

Post-Civil War

- 13th – abolishes slavery [1865]
- 14th – guaranteed citizenship; all citizens guaranteed due process of law and equal protection of the law; federal gov't would protect rights if stated failed to do so (at least in theory; many states didn't follow this, and it took the Civil Rights movement to enforce it. For this reason, this is one of the most important post-Bill of Rights amendments). [1868]
- 15th – cannot be deprived the right to vote based on race or being a former slave (ways to get around this though such as literacy tests, poll taxes, grandfather clause, etc.) [1870]

Progressive Era

- 16th – federal income tax [1913]
- 17th – direct election of Senators (as opposed to being elected by state legislatures)
  - original design was to help prevent mobocracy or allowing the common people to directly elect someone like…themselves! [1913]
- 18th – prohibition of manufacture or sale of alcohol (Prohibition) [1919]
- 19th – gave women the right to vote [1920]

More modern

- 21st – repeals (cancels) the 18th amendment (cancels Prohibition) [1933]; during the Great Depression
- 22nd – limited the President to two terms or 10 years in office [1951]; after FDR's four terms
- 24th – abolished poll taxes (taxes to vote) [1964]; during Civil Rights movement
- 26th – guaranteed the right to vote for all citizens 18 years and older [1971]; during the Vietnam War; if you're old enough to fight, you're old enough to vote

Most Important Supreme Ct. Cases

- Most important Chief Justice was John Marshall (served 1801 – 1835) who helped shape the courts early years and set many of its precedents; strong nationalist sentiment, that is, he established the supremacy of national government over the states
- The 2nd most important chief Justice was probably Earl Warren (served 1953 – 1969). His court presided over many of the decisions that affect our modern society today.

- 1803 – *Marbury v. Madison* = judicial review
- 1819 – *McCulloch v. Maryland* – Maryland (state) could not tax the Bank of the U.S. (national) – placed federal/national power over the states
- 1824 – *Gibbons v. Ogden* – states cannot regulate interstate commerce; again, federal power trumps state power in these situations
- 1857 – *Dred Scott v. Sanford* decision – slaves are not citizens but property. Therefore, the government cannot regulate where slavery can spread since property rights are protected.
- 1896 – *Plessy v. Ferguson* – established the idea of "separate but equal"; based on Homer Plessy's desire to ride a train in the white section even though he was 1/8 black.
- 1908 – *Muller v. Oregon* – ruled that women's work hours could be regulated/restricted because they deserved special treatment. Although it seems like gender discrimination, it was considered progressive at the time because it actually gave women some protection from harsh employers who could otherwise work women relentlessly.
- 1919 – *Schenck v. United States* – In this case, the Supreme Court approved the Espionage/Sedition Acts of WWI; freedom of expression can be restricted if it demonstrates a "clear and present danger" (like shouting fire in a crowded theater)
- 1944 – *Korematsu v. United States* – upheld the constitutionality of the Japanese internment camps
- 1962 – *Engle v. Vitale* – made it illegal for states/schools to require prayer in schools
- 1963 – *Gideon v. Wainright* – guaranteed an accused a lawyer if they can't afford one
- 1964 – *Reynolds v. Simms* – ruled that state legislature districts had to be more or less equal in representation. Representatives in power would try to draw the district maps so that many poor, urban areas were in one district and split up rural areas so as to give them more power.
- 1966 – *Miranda v. Arizona* – guaranteed the accused would be read their rights ("You have the right to remain silent…"
- 1973 – *Roe v. Wade* – states cannot make abortion illegal (still controversial to this day with people choosing the pro – life or pro – choice camps)
- 1978 – *Univ. of CA (*at Berkeley) *v. Bakke* – ruled that race could be a factor but not the factor when using quotas for affirmative action purposes; Bakke was white and claimed it was "reverse discrimination"

Political Parties in U.S. History

	Federalists	Democratic Republicans (former anti-feds)
1790s – early 1800s	Hamilton Favored strong central gov't Loose construction (interpretation of the Constitution) For a National Bank Pro-British Favored cities, commercial class More prominent in the Northeast	Jefferson Favored more power in the states Strict construction (interpretation) Opposed to a National Bank Pro-French Favored farmers, rural More prominent in the South
	In this early era, it was typical to have fear and distrust of too much democracy, or the development of a "mobocracy" of the common people (especially on the part of the Federalists), so there were property qualifications to vote in elections	
	Whigs	Jacksonian Democrats
1830s and 1840s	Hamiltonian ideas Commercial/business interests Strong/involved central gov't Supported roads/canals (American System) Opposed slavery expansion Variety of groups but united in their opposition of Jackson and his party	Jeffersonian ideas of limited gov't Small farmers States should have more control Pro – slavery Limited gov't
	By the 1830s, with the coming of the Era of the common man, parties and their candidates were courting the average voter a great deal more, emphasizing their humble "log cabin" roots, even if not true. To be associated with too much wealth, and to snub the common people, was now negative.	
	Republicans (start in 1854) (mostly in the North and West)	Democrats (mostly in the South)
2nd half of 19th century	Opposed the spread of slavery Pro – business and high tariffs to protect them Supported the gold standard Strong central gov't	Pro – slavery / segregation States rights Farmer based Opposed the gold standard (silver in 1896!)
	See the Progressive Era (1900 – 1920) for the effects of Progressivism on government involvement	
	Republicans	Democrats
1930s – present (Keep in mind, these are generalizations!)	Pro – business (1920s too) Favors small gov't Conservative Laissez faire Strong against communism; Emphasis on defense	Pro – regulation of business Favors larger gov't to create safety nets, etc. (see FDR and New Deal, subsequent Great Society in the 1960s) Liberal Strong against communism; not as strong on defense near end of 20th century

Significant 3rd Parties in U.S. History

Liberty and Free Soil Parties (1840s – 50s)	• Originated from anti-slavery members from the two major parties • Opposed the spread of slavery not on grounds of immorality but rather practicality; slavery in new territories represented competition with free whites; • "Free soil, free speech, free labor and free men" • Remnants merged with the Republican Party hodgepodge in the 1850s
Know – Nothing Party 1840s, 1850s	• Focused on nativism (anti – immigrant and anti – Catholic backlash to the waves of Old immigrants, especially Irish and Germans) • A.k.a. "Order of the Star – Spangled Banner" • Mostly big in the Northeast, where many immigrants were arriving…
Populist Party (People's Party) (1890s)	• Mostly made up of farmers who were angry because of the hold that big business and railroads had over them • Wanted free coinage of silver (would create inflation; good for farmers) • Desired public ownership of railroads, grain elevators, etc. – that way they could be regulated (it's "in the public good" they'd argue) • The height of the movement was William Jennings Bryan's "Cross of Gold" speech call to arms against big business (unfortunately for the Populists, WJB ran as a Democrat and that party took over the Populist agenda and they gradually died out) • Lastly, the whole movement failed because they could not get workers in the cities to join forces with the farmers
Progressive Party (Bull Moose Party) 1912 Election and briefly beyond	• Because TR was disappointed in Taft as a reformer, he ran in this 3rd party • He championed many Progressive causes: regulation of big business and its alliance with corrupt politics, greater democracy, campaign reform, women's suffrage • The result was to split the Republican vote and give the election to Woodrow Wilson (Still, this was the most successful third party in modern U.S. history with TR winning more votes than Taft!) • Robert LaFollette – the fighting governor of Wisconsin carried the party on for a couple of elections but it was declining by 1924
Dixiecrats of 1948	• After Truman angered Southerners with the desegregation of the armed forces in 1948 and other civil rights progress, the States' Rights Democratic Party (a.k.a. the Dixiecrats) was formed • Favored States' rights and limiting civil rights legislation • Strom Thurmond (long standing S. Carolina politician) was their nominee for President • Nearly cost Truman the election of 1948 and was the beginning of the gradual dissolution of the "Solid South" as a Democratic voting bloc
American Independent Party (George Wallace)	• Focused on a segregationist platform for the election of 1968 • Nominated Alabama Governor George Wallace as their candidate • Conservative party and representative of segregationist portions of the South as well as the backlash to the liberal changes of the 1960s

Epic U.S. History Review

Miscellaneous sections

Examples of limits/violations of rights by the federal government
- Alien/Sedition Acts (1798)
- Lincoln's suspension of the writ of habeas corpus during the Civil War
- Espionage (1917) and Sedition (1918) Acts during WWI
- Internment of Japanese Americans during WWII (1942 – 1944)

History of Temperance/Prohibition
- Temperance – movement to reduce/end drinking of alcohol
- Alcohol is seen as ruining many families; caused injuries in factories; "demon rum"
- Women were often heavily involved in the temperance movements as were churches (especially women **in** churches!)
- American Temperance Society (Founded 1826)
- T.S. Arthur wrote a book called, "Ten Nights in a Barroom and What I Saw There" (1854) dramatizing the terrible effects of alcohol on a small town
- Neil S. Dow, known as the "Father of Prohibition," helped pass the Maine Law (1851); Maine became the first state to prohibit the sale and manufacture of alcohol
- Women's Christian Temperance Union (WCTU) (1873) – led by Frances Willard during the Progressive Era – more about promoting temperance and morality than legal prohibition (convince people alcohol is evil)
- Anti – Saloon League (1893) – more about prohibition through political means (make alcohol illegal in states, counties, etc.)
- Carrie A. Nation – a tall grandmother who would smash bottles in saloons with her hatchet. Many bars had a sign that said, "All nations welcome but Carrie."
- 18th amendment (1919) – prohibition of manufacture or sale of alcohol (Prohibition)
  - Known as the "noble experiment"
  - Volstead Act – name of the law that actually enforced the 18th amendment and gave specifics as to how it would actually work
  - Generally failed to significantly reduce drinking on a national scale
  - Led to an increase of organized crime
- 21st amendment (1933) – repealed the 18th amendment because of the above reasons and because during the Great Depression, the government would rather tax a legal industry than lose all that potential revenue to an illegal business

Art
- Early – mid 1800s – Hudson River Art School
  - Focused on landscapes and natural beauty; "romanticized ideals"; era of Transcendentalism
- American art of the 1800s began to differentiate itself from European art
  - Western themes; Native Americans
- Early 20th Century – The Ashcan School
  - Focused on realism
  - Harsh realities of daily life as opposed to the earlier Romantacism
- Georgia O'Keefe – 1920s and beyond – She is one of the most famous of American painters
  - Focused on Southwestern themes

- Post WWII and modern
  - Abstract Expressionism – Jack Pollock
  - Normal Rockwell - Famous for producing paintings of American culture. He illustrated the cover of a popular magazine called the Saturday Evening Post for decades.
  - Andy Warhol – probably the most famous artist in the last 50 years. He popularized "pop art" – pushing boundaries of expression; often used famous subjects including Marilyn Monroe, Elvis, and Campbell's Soup cans

Literature - Far too broad and hard to really capture if you're not actually reading the books, but here is a bare minimum highlights…
- Ralph Waldo Emerson and Henry David Thoreau (Walden, Civil Disobedience) …themes: nonconformist, individualistic, self-reliance, opposed to organized religion, optimistic
- "Anti – Transcendentalists"
  - Nathaniel Hawthorne (the Scarlet Letter) focused on dark allegories and psychology
  - Herman Melville (Moby Dick) also emphasized these tragic and dark themes. Man vs. nature, etc…
- Horatio Alger Jr. – He wrote books primarily about boys who rose from humble and difficult circumstances to success through hard work and good values. He had a dramatic effect on attitudes during the Gilded Age.
- Other 1800s notables: Poets Walt Whitman and Emily Dickinson and author Mark Twain
- Lost Generation of the 1920s – F. Scott Fitzgerald (The Great Gatsby), Ernest Hemingway (The Old Man and the Sea) and others
  - Disillusioned after WWI, these authors/ poets rejected the materialism of the booming 1920s
- Harlem Renaissance – First major opportunity for literary self-expression for African Americans
  - Langston Hughes was the most notable poet of the H.R.
- John Steinbeck – Wrote during the Great Depression so many of his books involve social criticism
  - Grapes of Wrath – his most famous novel, about a desperate family that travels from OK to CA fleeing the Dust Bowl and the struggles and injustices they face as a poor family during the Great Depression
  - Other Steinbeck novels: Of Mice and Men, Cannery Row, and East of Eden
- Beatniks – In the 1950s, a group of intellectuals and poets who expressed dissatisfaction with the status quo and were the beginning of the counterculture movement; experimentation with drugs was also a component of this
  - Jack Kerouac – On the Road (one of the more famous books of the time)
  - Compare with the Lost Generation of the 20s
- 50s – 70s heyday of American Literature
  - Harper Lee – To Kill a Mockingbird
  - Joseph Heller's – Catch-22
  - Kurt Vonnegut Jr. – Slaughterhouse-Five
  - J.D. Salinger – The Catcher in the Rye
  - Ralph Ellison – Invisible Man

Books/writings to know:
- Common Sense (1776) – Thomas Paine – why the colonies should be independent
- The Federalist (papers) (1787 – 88) – by Alexander Hamilton, James Madison, John Jay – series of essays/arguments to convince people to accept the new Constitution
- Civil Disobedience (1849) – by Henry David Thoreau – resistance against injustice
- Uncle Tom's Cabin (1852) – Harriet Beecher Stowe – powerful abolition novel
- Ten Nights in a Barroom and What I Saw There (1854) – T.S. Arthur – temperance novel
- A Century of Dishonor (1881) – Helen Hunt Jackson – criticism of government dealings with American Indians
- Influence of Sea Power on History (1890) – Alfred T. Mahan – importance of strong navy/bases and controlling the seas to have an empire.

Progressive Muckraker books
- How the Other Half Lives (1890) – Jacob Riis – about the poor/slums late 1800s, early 1900s
- Shame of the Cities (1904) – Lincoln Steffens – articles in McClure's about government corruption in cities
- History of the Standard Oil Company (1904) – Ida Tarbell – exposed Rockefeller's practices
- The Jungle (1906) – Upton Sinclair – exposed disgusting meatpacking practices

Others
- Mein Kampf (1925 – 26) – "My Struggle" – Hitler's powerful book outlining his ideas
- Silent Spring (1962) – Rachel Carson – about how modern society is damaging the environment; helped to launch modern environmentalism
- The Feminine Mystique (1963) – Betty Friedan – questioned the role of women and conservative expectations of the 1950s. Helped spark the modern feminist movement.

General Terms/Vocabulary To Know / Keep Straight

- annex – to attach, add onto, or incorporate into. This last one is the best use for U.S. History purposes as in the annexation of Texas or Hawaii. This is when these states are incorporated into being a part of the United States.
- appeasement – to give into the demands of a belligerent (warlike/aggressive) nation; often hoping this will satisfy them (see Hitler and WWII)
- arsenal – a place to store weapons; a supplier of weapons (see John Brown in 1859)
- assimilation – to absorb or conform to the customs, languages, and practices of the dominant society/nation. In U.S. History, this is usually used in terms of immigrants and American Indians. The process can be gradual and done willingly or by forced assimilation (e.g. when American Indian children were taken from their parents and put into American schools). The term "Westernization" also refers to the process of becoming more like the Western civilization (i.e. European and American). E.g. "they are gradually westernizing…"
- domestic policy – how the gov't deals with problems at home (within the U.S.)
  - o vs. foreign policy – how the gov't deals with international or foreign problems
- enfranchise – be given the right to vote (disenfranchised can mean to lose the right to vote)

- <u>inter</u>state commerce/roads, etc. – trade or roads that cross <u>between</u> states – important because only Congress has the authority to regulate interstate affairs
- <u>intra</u>state – that which stays <u>within</u> the state – therefore is controlled by that state
- patronage – can mean to financially support a business, but for U.S. History purposes, the important definition is similar to the Spoils System – handing out jobs in return for political support
- secede – to withdraw from (not succeed)
- subsidy – government aid given to private businesses or individuals. This can be in many forms: cash, land, tax breaks, etc. In the 1800s, the U.S. gov't subsidized the railroad industry by giving them huge expanses of land in exchange for building the RRs (this benefits the gov't by providing a means for which its people can settle the West and transport goods, thus benefitting the economy). Today, people talk about the controversies of oil companies and farmers getting subsidized by the federal gov't (i.e. getting tax breaks to develop oil supplies or not plant crops) and individuals getting subsidized with free or reduced health care and food stamps,etc.
- suffrage – right to vote
- tariff (duty) – a tax on imported (foreign) goods;
  - excise – a tax on internal (non-foreign) products, usually things like alcohol and tobacco
  - duty – another word for tax; if you go to international airports, you'll likely see ads for "duty free shopping" meaning tax-free shopping (prices are probably heavily marked up though!).
- war hawk – someone who favors war (as opposed to a "dove" who favors peace)
- xenophobia – fear/hatred of foreigners; (therefore, a xenophobe is similar to a nativist)

31801051R00048